ACHIEVING SCHOOL READINESS

Public Libraries and National Education

GOAL NO.1

With a "Prototype of Public Library Services for Young Children and Their Families"

Edited by

Barbara Froling Immroth

and

Viki Ash-Geisler

American Library Association

Chicago and London

1995

The paper used in this publication meets the minimum requirements of American National Standard for Information Sciences—Permanence of Paper for Printed Library Materials, ANSI Z39.48-1992.

Project Manager: David Epstein
Cover design: Tessing Design
Text design: Dianne M. Rooney
Composition by Publishing Services, Inc.,
    in ITC Caslon 224 on Xyvision/Linotype.
Printed on 50-pound Thor, a pH-neutral stock,
    and bound in 10 pt CIS by Mallory Lithographing, Inc.

Library of Congress Cataloging-in-Publication Data
Achieving school readiness : public libraries and national education goal
    no. 1 / [edited] by Barbara Froling Immroth and Viki Ash-Geisler.
        p.   cm.
    Results of an institute held at the Graduate School of Library and
    Information Science at the University of Texas at Austin, May 1994.
    Includes bibliographical references and index.
    ISBN 0-8389-0649-4 (alk. paper)
    1. Public libraries—United States—Services to preschool children—
    Congresses.   2. Readiness for school—United States—Congresses.
    I. Immroth, Barbara Froling.   II. Ash-Geisler, Viki.   III. American
    Library Association.
    Z718.2.U6A24   1995
    027.62′5′0973—dc20   94-49145
                                                                        CIP

Printed in the United States of America

99 98 97 96 95   5 4 3 2 1

*Dedicated to active and
engaged learners of all ages*

CONTENTS

ACKNOWLEDGMENTS

Thanks are due in large measure to the Office of Library Programs, U.S. Department of Education, for entrusting us with the Title II B grant that made this work possible. Ray Fry, Director, Christina Dunn, and Louise Sutherland have each given sound advice and encouragement along the way—from writing the proposal to administering the grant, organizing the Achieving School Readiness Institute, and compiling, editing, and publishing these papers.

Brooke Sheldon, Dean of the Graduate School of Library and Information Science, University of Texas at Austin, gave both time and support to this project from its inception. The GSLIS office staff have expended considerable energy on the additional demands of the project.

Institute participants continue to refine, publicize, and promote a new vision of library service to young children. Their contributions not only to the prototype, but to the future of public library service, are both commended and appreciated. Unfailing enthusiasm and good humor during long work sessions and thoughtful consideration of several prototype drafts have been the hallmarks of this cooperative and collaborative group.

Virginia Mathews, ALA Honorary Member, author, editor, and activist for children's services, spoke about the history and development of public library children's service, and emphasized the importance of partnerships with others, especially the Library/Head Start Partnership. She participated in the development of the prototype and shared her leadership experience and expertise. Her personal vision of the importance of youth advocates' active participation in political and social arenas is included as a Coda to this volume.

Margaret Kimmel, professor at the School of Library and Information Science, University of Pittsburgh, Oralia Garza de Cortes, Austin Public Library, and Sherry Des Enfants, DeKalb County Public Library, spun a magical web of stories that brought the oral traditions of the past to contemporary library concerns.

Oralia Garza de Cortes, Austin Public Library, Frances Dowd, Texas Woman's University, Penny Markey, County of Los Angeles Public Library, Janice Smuda, Cuyahoga County (Ohio) Public Library, and Caroline Ward, Nassau (New York) Library System, offered inspirational insights through presentations on exemplary library programs for preschoolers.

Jim Scheppke, State Librarian of Oregon, where children's service is the priority, and Elizabeth Morgan, Director of Connections, an Austin community resource center for child care professionals and parents, each added rich dimensions to the development of the prototype.

The editors extend their heartfelt appreciation to each of these individuals for their invaluable assistance.

INTRODUCTION

Libraries and the National Education Goals

The National Education Goals were established by President George Bush and the governors of the fifty states in 1989. The Clinton administration adopted the goals and successfully integrated them into federal law in March 1994 as the Goals 2000: Educate America Act, Public Law 103–227. Numerous popular and professional articles have been written about the National Education Goals since the Governor's Conference in 1989.

As is often the case in discussions of education policy, libraries have not figured prominently. Several documents written by librarians, however, address the issue of libraries as they relate to supporting and furthering the National Education Goals. In *Libraries for the National Education Goals,*

BARBARA FROLING IMMROTH is professor at the Graduate School of Library and Information Science, University of Texas at Austin. She authored "A Background Paper written in preparation for an Update of the Fast Response Survey System Services and Resources for Children in Public Libraries, 1988–89 . . ." at the request of the Office of Library Programs, U.S. Department of Education, Office of Educational Research and Improvement. She served as president of the Association for Library Service to Children. She was Director of the Achieving School Readiness Institute.

VIKI ASH-GEISLER is a doctoral candidate at the Graduate School of Library and Information Science, University of Texas at Austin, and a Title II B Fellow. Her research interests center on public library service to preschool children in child care settings. She was formerly the Coordinator of Children's Services at the Corpus Christi (Texas) Public Library and has served as Chair of the Texas Library Association Children's Roundtable. She acted as Coordinator of the Achieving School Readiness Institute.

Stripling (1992) supplies extensive documentation about how libraries are contributing to education in the United States. "Implementing the National Goals for Education through Library Service," a position paper of the American Library Association (ALA), presents a statement of major contributions that librarians and libraries can make to achieve the goals and also gives examples of specific library programs and services that are furthering the goals achievement. Prepared by a Task Force representing six ALA divisions, this position paper was used at the 1991 White House Conference on Library and Information Service (WHCLIS); it was also submitted to the National Goals Evaluation Panel as part of written testimony prepared by ALA outlining contributions that libraries make to education.

The National Education Goals, along with the major contribution of libraries outlined in "Implementing the National Goals for Education through Library Service," are:

GOAL 1

By the year 2000, all children in America will start school ready to learn.

Major contribution: Librarians and library programs work with children, adults serving the child, and parents to provide materials and prereading experiences that prepare children to enter and remain in school (American Library Association 1991, p. 331).

GOAL 2

By the year 2000, the high school graduation rate will increase to at least 90 percent.

Major contribution: Libraries serve as resource centers for teachers, students, and parents in support of and as an extension of all curricular activities (ALA 1991, p. 332).

GOAL 3

By the year 2000, American students will leave grades four, eight, and twelve having demonstrated competency in challenging subject matter including English, mathematics, science, history, and geography; and every school in America will ensure that all students learn to use their minds well, so they may be prepared for responsible citizenship, further earning, and productive employment in our modern economy.

Major contribution: Librarians help students develop lifelong learning habits and the ability to use information effectively (ALA 1991, p. 332).

GOAL 4

By the year 2000, American students will be first in the world in science and mathematics achievement.

Major contribution: Librarians, as information specialists, facilitate students' access to advanced information and research (ALA 1991, p. 333).

GOAL 5

By the year 2000, every adult American will be literate and will possess the knowledge and skills necessary to compete in a global economy and exercise the rights and responsibilities of citizenship.

Major contributions: To promote lifelong learning skills, libraries encourage reading for leisure, research for self-improvement, and economic advancement. Library collections provide access to materials that reflect ever-changing global events as well as historical materials (ALA 1991, p. 333).

GOAL 6

By the year 2000, every school in America will be free of drugs and violence and will offer a disciplined environment conducive to learning.

Major contribution: Libraries provide current information on many issues including substance abuse and other societal problems. In addition, libraries offer a neutral setting for children and adults to seek information in dealing with difficult problems (ALA 1991, p. 333).

The First Goal

Acknowledging the need to make preschool children a national priority, the *National Education Goals Report, 1992* states that "in pursuing a common mission to nurture America's youngest citizens, we become a stronger society. And young children growing up in such a society, where childhood is protected and enriched, will be ready—even eager—to learn" (p. 8). The report goes on to acknowledge that assessing readiness for school is a difficult task. "Being ready to learn means more than having the ability to count and recognize letters in the alphabet. Children need to be healthy, and socially and emotionally ready for school." (p. 8) While there are no specific, objective measures of readiness to learn, the National Education Goals Panel has identified five critical dimensions that define school readiness. These dimensions include:

1. Physical Well-being and Motor Development

   Health and physical growth, ranging from being rested, fed, properly immunized, and healthy to having such abilities as running, jumping, and using crayons and puzzles.

2. Social and Emotional Development

   The sense of personal well-being that allows a child to participate fully and constructively in classroom activities.

3. Approaches Toward Learning

   The curiosity, creativity, motivation, independence, cooperativeness, interest, and persistence that enable children from all cultures to maximize their learning.

4. Language Usage

   The talking, listening, scribbling, and composing that enable children to communicate effectively and express thoughts, feelings, and experiences.

5. Cognition and General Knowledge

   Familiarity with basic information—including patterns and relationships, and cause and effect—needed to solve problems in everyday life.

(*National Education Goals Report*, 1992, p. 9)

Achieving School Readiness Institute

In May of 1994 the Graduate School of Library and Information Science at the University of Texas at Austin held a five-day Institute titled "Achieving School Readiness: Public Libraries and the First of the National Education Goals." Funded by a Title IIB grant from the U.S. Department of Education, the Institute brought together a national group of state library and education consultants, early childhood educators, library school faculty, library system coordinators, and practicing children's librarians. (See the Appendix for a complete roster of Institute participants.) The purpose of the Institute was three-fold:

1. to broaden understanding of the five critical dimensions of school readiness
2. to examine the services provided to preschool children in the nation's public libraries in light of that understanding
3. to develop and disseminate a prototype of library service to preschool children to assist in achievement of Goal 1.

While it is impossible to capture in print the excitement and enthusiasm that developed during the Institute, the sense of camaraderie and collective concern shared by librarians and members of the early care and education community that permeated the Institute finds a voice in the prototype itself. The shared experience of reflecting on the theories and research of early childhood provided a unique opportunity to apply new insights to a vision of children's library service. It is the intent of this volume to share with a national audience the knowledge that was gained during the Institute and the results of the collaborative effort of developing the prototype.

Chapter Content

In the first chapter, "On Becoming a Natural-Born Story-teller," Vivian Gussin Paley describes the joy of finding her own voice as a storyteller through a growing awareness of the storytelling lives of her students. A master teacher at the

University of Chicago Laboratory School, Paley enlivens her paper not only with her own original stories, but with the voices of children in vignettes from the doll corner and the block area of her kindergarten classroom.

Dr. Stuart Reifel addresses physical well-being and motor development in Chapter Two, "Preschool Play: Some Roots for Literacy." Drawing upon the work of Piaget and Vygotsky and citing current research studies, Reifel suggests that the physical activities identified as play are the "context within which children learn, explore, and acquire foundations that they will draw upon later in school." Reifel maintains that play is a significant means for developing cognitive structures, enhancing social development, and exploring symbolic thought. In relating play specifically to the library and literacy, Reifel says "Hearing stories (a social activity) gives us something to play about. Playing (frequently a social activity) allows us to create stories." He concludes with the suggestion that libraries develop "playful, welcoming environments where children can explore and imagine with books" and that librarians help children to "play appropriately in libraries."

The dimension of social and emotional development is considered by Dr. Alice Sterling Honig in Chapter Three, "Children's Socioemotional Development: Implications for School Readiness." She begins with the premise that "intellectual abilities of children and their potential for school readiness and early learning can be optimized only when their emotional security, self-esteem, and social supports from intimate others are nurtured along with their cognitive competence." Although children, from infancy, exhibit certain temperament types and patterns of emotional response, their understanding of the range and complexity of emotions is not quick to develop and can be enhanced or hampered by their adult caregivers. For this reason, Honig suggests that libraries can be invaluable resources of materials and programs for promoting "effective parenting and thus children's positive socioemotional development."

Dr. Karen H. Nelson explores approaches to learning in Chapter Four, "Learning Styles in Preschool Children." She stresses that contemporary research is utilizing sophisticated techniques for assessing the physiological reality of learning style and its behavioral implications. The literature argues that we must accept diversity in style, Nelson emphasizes, with no single style model purported to explain broad individual differences in learning; that style is being examined in relation to (1) temperament; (2) intellectual ability; (3) developmental status. In regard to the delivery of library programs to preschool children, Nelson advises librarians to increase their sensitivity to the variety of learning styles that their audiences display, while avoiding efforts to assess or label children according to style. Rather than "worrying about the child's style," Nelson recommends, "think instead about ways in which you can use diverse styles in your presentations in hopes that once in a while a child whose parent or teacher has a different style may discover that there is a style that affirms who she is."

Dr. Sarah Hudelson addresses language usage in Chapter Five, "Preschool Children's Oral and Written Language: Issues and Challenges." She summarizes current research on young children's oral and written language acquisition, emphasizing that children coming to school have already acquired a high degree of linguistic competence that reflects the values and culture of the speech communities in which they live. Even among native speakers of English, Hudelson maintains that there is "significant variation in the ways in which families and communities use oral and written language." It is the responsibility of the teacher and the librarian to acknowledge what children already know about language and to understand and respect the diversity of language styles that children bring to the preschool setting.

In Chapter Six, Dr. William Teale addresses general knowledge and cognition in "Public Libraries and Emergent Literacy: Helping Set the Foundation for School Success." He focuses on the characteristics of positive literacy environments for young children in home, community, and library settings. Highlighting storybook reading, playing with language, and literacy play activities, Teale suggests that each contributes to children's knowledge and cognitive development and to their success in school. "The key," he claims, "lies in children seeing literacy as an enjoyable and valued part of their lives. We help them see this not by devising literacy lessons but by helping to create contexts in which children experience the power and joy of reading and writing."

The Prototype

Finally, Chapter Seven summarizes the small-group work accomplished by the Institute participants in creating the "Prototype of Public Library Services for Young Children and Their Families," the text of which then follows.

The prototype, which addresses services, attitudes and skills, organizational structures, and resources, is not intended as a checklist for individual libraries or librarians. It is instead, an attempt to engage the widest cross section of the library community. Library educators, administrators, practitioners, and supporters, must all work together in pursuit of exemplary service to young children and their families. According to Senator Jeff Bingaman of New Mexico, ". . . ensuring that [all children] begin school ready to learn will take a national commitment, including leadership from the very top, to make preschool children a priority" (*National Education Goals Report 1992*, p. 8).

The prototype, Virginia Mathew's passionate "Call to Action" following it, and this publication as a whole can be seen as part of the effort to bring this priority, service to preschool children, to the nation's public libraries.

Works Cited

American Library Association. (1991). Implementing the national goals for education through library service. *Journal of Youth Services in Libraries, 4,* 331–334.

National education goals report, 1992: Executive summary. (1993). Washington, DC: National Education Goals Committee.

Stripling, B. K. (1992). *Libraries for the national education goals.* Syracuse, NY: ERIC Clearinghouse on Information Resources.

CHAPTER 1

On Becoming a Natural-Born Storyteller

VIVIAN GUSSIN PALEY

For many years I did not know that my classrooms were occupied by natural-born storytellers who plied their trade while they played. Having been told in college that play is the work of children, I was curious about this activity, but seldom did I listen to its language the way we do when someone tells a story.

"Pretend I'm a kitty and pretend I'm lost," a child might say, "and then you find me and we hear a noise, only we don't know what it is." This child has good social skills, I would note, passing right by the daily invention of literature with hardly a nod of recognition.

Yet, until I perceived the children as storytellers, I was unable to become one myself, and this is what I longed to be. Oh, not a Beatrix Potter or E. B. White, but I did so want to make up little stories to help bridge those awkward transitions school is full of, the unplanned moments when our connec-

VIVIAN GUSSIN PALEY is on the faculty at the University of Chicago Laboratory School where she has taught for over thirty years. Her books about the teaching-learning process include: *You Can't Say You Can't Play, Boys and Girls: Superheroes in the Doll Corner* and *Wally's Stories.* Recipient of the Erikson Institute Award in 1987, Paley was named a MacArthur Fellow in 1989.

tions to each other seem blurred, and even the most familiar book too distant.

The children, of course, will jump bravely into such a void, resurrecting earlier disguises ("Now you be Batman and I'm Joker"), but these noisy interludes were not what I had in mind. Little did I suspect that these children and I shared similar goals: the use of fantasy to calm our anxieties and re-assemble ourselves along promising new paths.

There I was, reading as many good books to the class as I could and not wondering what these excellent stories had to do with the children's play or with my own restlessness in the classroom. Like the person who does not stop to smell the flowers, I barely paused to listen to the narratives blooming everywhere in the garden of children where I spent my days.

Since I no longer recalled my own early fantasies and was not ready to savor the gifts of the storytellers in my midst, how could I become a teller of stories? Apparently neither the children's play nor the books we read were enough to help me find my way back to what, as a child, I had accomplished without self-consciousness or effort.

It was not simply that I paid too little attention to the spontaneous scripts that sprouted like dandelions whenever the children played. The matter was more complex. I mistook the relationship between play and the books we read, not real-izing that both emerge from the same source.

Pretend, as the children are prone to say, that I am read-ing *Cinderella,* and immediately afterwards some of its char-acters appear in the doll corner. "Scrub the floor! You can't go to the ball!" they shout. None of this surprises me, of course. The children are doing what they are programmed to do: re-produce the stories they hear.

Never mind the nuances and ploys not in the original text. "If you don't let me go to the ball, I won't invite you to my birthday!" "I'm not the mean sister, I'm the baby." Are the children simply copying a story? Doesn't it sound instead as if they are expanding and deepening its underlying themes, perhaps even inventing a new story? These would have been useful questions but I did not ask them.

Much later I would understand that the fairy tales, televi-sion shows—yes, even that clever spider Charlotte and the worrisome Peter Rabbit—all come from the same place as the children's play. The impetus for arranging ideas into story form is not uniquely the province of book writers but, in truth, belongs to us all. And, furthermore, it is a talent that begins at the beginning, the natural birthright of children.

For, surely, as soon as there are words enough and society enough and time enough, the stories are there. Children are ready to tell their stories and listen to ours long before school begins. If the terms *ready* or *readiness* have any meaning in regard to school, it is to be found first in the inner and outer monologues of children at play as they begin to socialize in a storytelling community. To ignore this is akin to planning an automobile journey without the fuel.

Now, let us return to the girls in the doll corner acting out *Cinderella*. How do they know that the mean stepsisters can't come to a birthday? Or that, deprived of a loving mother, Cinderella shall be given a baby sister? Because the issues in fairy tales are the ordinary stuff of doll corner play: loss (a mother's death); fear (the threat of abandonment); jealousy (siblings vying for preferred status); joy (a ball, like a birthday, represents pleasure and power); danger (retribution follows too much joy); and, of course, vindication (good sisters are rewarded and bad sisters punished).

The children know, far better than we do, that heroes come with many faces. Here is a version of *Cinderella*, filtered through layers of silk scarves, as two five-year-olds dress up in the doll corner:

Janine: You be the baby. I'm the big sister.

Sarah: Pretend there are two big sisters. The baby is dead.

Janine: The baby is lost and the mother . . .

Sarah: How about pretend the baby is crying in the woods and a mother bear says, "What's the matter, baby? Are your sisters mean?"

Janine: Don't be the sisters are mean. The mother is mean.

Sarah: Pretend mean?

Janine: Pretend I'm the mother and I look for the
            baby because there are footsteps.
Sarah: And I'm the good fairy, I mean the mother
            bear, but I pretend to be a fairy to go to the
            ball.
Janine: Is there a ball?
Sarah: Sure, because the baby is really Cinderella.
            Okay. I'll be the baby.

Which Cinderella came first, the one sitting by the ashes
or the baby lost in the woods? Come to think of it, which
came first, *The Three Pigs* who build their separate houses
or a story about a mother who prefers the baby to its older
brothers, as described in the following sandtable drama?

Jeremy: The mother lives in here. In this hole.
Stanley: The baby bear want to come in. Let me in, let
            me in.
Jeremy: No babies. She said go away. Too crowded.
            Make your own house over there.
Stanley: Then she can't be a mother.
Jeremy: I mean, I forgot, she really locked the door on
            the other brothers, not the baby. Come in,
            come in. Those guys have to build another
            house. Not a brick one. We have the brick
            house, you and me, not them.

What a convenient way to get rid of older siblings and
cement a friendship besides! Are you as surprised as I was
that *The Three Pigs* is really about mother-loves-baby best?
Perhaps, then, you'd like to know that the wolf is sometimes
a dad in disguise.

Amy: I got the cape. I'm Red Riding Girl. You have
            to be the wolf.
Sam: I'm not the bad guy.
Amy: He's really a dad. He pretends strong teeth.
Sam: Is he good?

Amy: Very good. He went away but then he came
            back when he got stronger like a wolf.

Amazingly, each plot, spontaneous and always in flux,
quickly arrives at the examination of a central concern. Fairy
tales and cartoons may provide some of the characters and actions but it is up to the children to carry them to new places.
Often the children's imagery precedes the adult product. I'm
told of a new movie called *Wolf,* about a mild-mannered man
who is bitten by a wolf and then turns "stronger like a wolf."
Did the screen writers steal their material from Amy and Sam?

No, it is not plagiarism; it is play. And clearly it is more
than just the work of children. One senses the beginnings of
human creativity and learning. Once upon a time, you see, all
these book and movie writers were children like those in our
preschools and kindergartens, making up stories every time
they played. Indeed, if we go back far enough we come to a
time when school had little if anything to do with the process.

Charlotte Brontë and her sisters and brother, for example,
did not attend school until the age of ten. These poor, mother-
less children played on the rugged English moors while their
bereaved father prepared his sermons; they created a world of
storytelling and story acting to make themselves feel safe and
loved. Charlotte and her siblings were left alone to tell each
other stories of being brave or afraid, best-loved or displaced,
dancing at the ball or sitting in the ashes. Do these not sound
like the origins of *Wuthering Heights* and *Jane Eyre*?

Today's children have not veered from the need to create
the same kinds of stories as filled the childhood days of the
Brontës. It must be noted, however, that any potential novel-
ists in our classrooms would be distracted and hampered
endlessly, all in the name of "readiness." We judge and pre-
judge, calling them "at-risk" and risky, if not worse, and, at
times, hardly seem to know what to do with these natural-
born storytellers. Even so, the children still manage to put
every question into story form and play out their mini-
narratives as if on a stage. Why did Daddy leave? Does
Mommy love the baby better than she loves me? Will I feel
safer as a powerful Ninja or a tiny baby? If Mr. McGregor
cooked me in a pie would Mommy cry for me?

Keisha: Where's that bad baby? I think Mr. McGregor cooked him.

Taylor: In a rabbit pie? Are we bunnies?

Keisha: Only Peter. Now we have to cry and then you say, don't be sad, Mommy loves you. Look! Here's Peter. You jumped out of the pot.

Jason: I'm not Peter anymore. I changed into a Ninja.

For whom did the Brontë children cry? I can see them in their mother's capes, roaming the moors, searching for a lost bunny or, perhaps, a lost princess. The losing and the finding is everything, isn't it? In telling a story we take from the barrage of confusing events that make us feel lost and weave some of the elements together along a single theme. Then we are safe for a while. And if we keep telling stories and playing them out we must inevitably arrive at the rainbow in the sky. Or at least it sometimes feels that way. In seeking the rainbow, we pursue the dramatic meanings ensconced in the events around us as we try to unscramble the images that crowd our minds. Then, one day, so suddenly it seems, this natural-born storytelling of ours comes to a halt.

My own childhood repertoire of stories disappeared as I grew older. I was well into my third decade of teaching when I felt ready once again to risk the role of storyteller. The children had to teach me their "work." The many hundreds of original stories acted out in a succession of doll corners, block areas, sandtables, and playgrounds crystallized into a format for my own storytelling only after the children began to dictate their stories to me and then perform them as if on a stage. The transposition of play on to the written page and then back into play—theater, we call it—created, finally, the connections I needed to revive my own beginnings.

Michelle: I can't find that boy Jack.

Danny: Pretend I'm Jack, but I don't want to climb the beanstalk.

Michelle: Do you climb it?

Danny: No, I just pretended because you were mean to me.

Michelle: I didn't let you . . .

Danny: You didn't let me stay home when I wanted.

Later in the day, Michelle ever so easily puts the doll corner drama into a story, and it becomes a natural extension of the original idea. "Once upon a time there was a mother and Jack. And the mother told Jack to climb up to see the rainbow. But Jack was too little, so the mother climbed up there and there was the rainbow fairy. So the mother changed to very beautiful and then she opened the door for Jack."

When at last I perceived children's play and storytelling as the track upon which all things make their first run, only then did I know that I too required this kind of continuity in the classroom. I wanted to experience what the children feel when they are deeply involved in a fantasy, those calming and satisfying emotional and intellectual consequences of making up stories. Being a schoolteacher, I found it natural to start with the subject of school itself, and I borrowed equally from the children and from Beatrix Potter. Later, I would invent my own heroes. For now I needed to build upon what was immediate and accessible.

One day when Peter Rabbit and his mother were taking a walk in the forest, she pointed to the tall oak trees and said, "Mrs. Owl thinks you will be ready for school when the leaves turn yellow and begin to fall." Peter gave the leaves a worried look. He wanted to stay home with his mother and little sisters. "But Mama," he said, "I can't go to school because they don't know what I look like."

"Mrs. Owl and the children will see you and then they will know," Mother Rabbit said. But Peter was still not sure he belonged in a place called school. "I can't go to school because they don't know my name," he said and his mother nodded her head. "We will tell them you are Peter Rabbit," she replied, "and then they will know."

Peter and his mother walked along and walked along and then Peter said, "But Mama, I don't know what the teacher does in school and I don't know what the children do."

Luckily for Peter, his mother knew. "One thing the teacher does is tell stories," Mother Rabbit said. "And another thing she does is help the children play." Peter thought about what his mother said. "And if someone pushes me?" he asked.

"Mrs. Owl will tell them to stop. And maybe it will remind her of a story. In fact, it reminds me of a story," said Peter's mother and, right then and there, while they walked along in the forest, Mother Rabbit began to tell Peter a story. "Once upon a time there was a little bird named Lulu who was in the habit of pushing her sisters and brothers out of the nest. 'I want this nest all to myself,' she told her mother. 'Won't you please make them another nest?' 'Very well,' replied the mother bird, 'since you can't stop pushing, that is exactly what I'll do.' So she built a second nest alongside the first and, lo and behold, a strange thing happened . . . ."

As you can see, there is no end to this natural-born story-telling once we begin. It gives us another voice, and this is what I had been missing. By now I had my teaching voice, used so often I barely heard myself. I had my reading voice, but the words were not my own. What I was uncovering was my storytelling voice, the one the children use when they play, the one I had brought to school sixty years earlier and lost somewhere along the way. If I had been able to continue telling my stories and even to act them out, might I have had the feeling I never had, that the people in school knew my face and my name?

Of one thing I was certain: this new voice of mine could help ease the pang of separation as the children and I set out to find whatever seemed lost. With it I could explain, complain, and sustain to my heart's content, and the children would not be afraid. Together we would build a brick house out of our interlocking narratives and no one would be left out. Furthermore, one day we would invite the parents and grandparents to bring their stories to school, for we needed them also to help explain who we are. In a storytelling community to explain who we are becomes a primary goal and source of nourishment.

Nearly everyone comes to school ready to understand a story. Johnny may not be able to sit still or color inside a circle; he may scramble the order of numbers up to ten or the letters in his name, but he can follow the complex struggles of the characters in our stories. He perceives their logic and motivation because he becomes one or all of them in turn.

Peter ran home from school, very upset. "A little squirrel named Emily knocked over my pile of acorns and I pushed her down and she cried," he told his mother. "Oh my," said Mother Rabbit. "Poor Emily and poor Peter. What did the teacher say?"

A tear rolled down Peter's face. "Mrs. Owl thinks it's my fault. She doesn't know Emily knocked down my acorns." Mother Rabbit sat Peter on her lap. "That reminds me of something that happened to me when I was little," she said. Peter dried his eyes and looked up at his mother. What could have happened to her that was like the awful thing that had just happened to him, he wondered.

Peter will find out and so will the children in my class, while I, their teacher, wander through the labyrinth of school experiences trying to remember what happened to me as a child. I'll place these images one by one, into the finest tool ever invented for examining cause and effect: the story. Then one day a new character will enter my storytelling, one I had never met before in any book or doll corner. A bird named Magpie will fly me to unexplored mountains and forests and I will then truly be able to join the children in their joyful work.

Magpie flew in the window and perched atop the big dictionary Schoolmistress kept on her desk. "What is your favorite word in this book?" he asked, fluffing his feathers.

"My favorite word?" Schoolmistress looked around at all the children busy with their lessons. "Why, Magpie, my favorite word is 'play', for that brings smiles to everyone's face. And after that, I like 'story' because that reminds us of play, don't you think?"

CHAPTER 2

Preschool Play
Some Roots for Literacy

STUART REIFEL

Before they enter the public schools, young children have a wide variety of experiences that provides a foundation for what they will later learn. Early experience provides a basis for cognitive, social, language, emotional, and physical development. Children grow and learn during these years by their contact with the world, including peers, physical objects, and the adults who supervise and guide them. What follows is a review of some of the research and theory we have to help us understand preschool experience. I will primarily address children's physical activity, their contact with objects and with other people. I will show how those contacts shape their thinking and development and how those contacts provide a foundation for understanding more about literacy, the world of words and books.

STUART REIFEL is associate professor of Early Childhood Education, Department of Curriculum and Instruction, University of Texas at Austin. His recent publications include "Sibling Play and Learning" in *Play and Culture,* and "Action, Talk, and Thought in the Block Corner" in *Play and the Social Context of Development in Early Care and Education.* He has worked in the Bing Nursery School, Stanford University, and as Head Teacher at the Lathrop Learning Center at Teachers College, Columbia University.

Much of a child's physical activity is play. Play is a context within which children learn, explore, and acquire foundations that they will draw on later in school. With this notion of play in mind, it will become clear that children are influenced by the objects they have in their homes and by experiences they have in preschool settings, as well as by other experiences in the broader community. Much of the preschool child's life is filled with play activities. In our society, play activities take many forms, such as playing in the sand, riding tricycles, building forts out of the cushions on a sofa, playing tag and peek-a-boo, and possibly watching television. Pretending to be characters we have seen in our real lives or characters we have seen on television is perhaps one of the most remarkable forms of play for many of us. There is a full range of possible play activities that tend to fill the lives of children, in their homes and in their many preschool programs, including child care. Over the past sixty years, a great deal of research has accumulated that shows us not only what that play looks like and how it develops, but also the significance of different aspects of play for development, including the development of cognitive abilities, language, peer relations, and other social understandings, as well as the development of physical abilities (Fein & Rivkin, 1986; Rubin, Fein, & Vandenberg, 1983; Smith, 1982).

Theories of Play and Development

Much of our thinking about play has been shaped by research done by Jean Piaget (1962). Piaget's description of the development of play provides one basis for many people's research on what young children do in their earliest years. For example, in his book, *Play, Dreams and Imitation in Childhood,* Piaget (1962) writes about the development of play through three broad stages.

Functional Play

Our youngest children, from infancy until age 18 months or so, are involved in a stage of play Piaget refers to as *functional* or *practice play.* This play is characterized by repeated actions on objects, such as when a child grabs and shakes a rattle. Another example might be when a child pushes a toy off the high chair to see it replaced by a caregiver, then pushes it off again, and again, and again.

By acting repeatedly on objects, children during this stage acquire an understanding of what the world is like. They begin to understand the qualities of objects, such as texture, size, weight, and contours. They also begin to understand how qualities might relate to one another, so that they can begin to form associations based on similarities. This kind of exploratory play with different objects, which includes having physical contact with many different types of objects in their environment, seems to provide a strong set of understandings from which the child can build later knowledge. The child appears to develop basic schemes to which he or she can later apply labels, such as hard, soft, round, square, red, yellow, and so on; from these they develop basic concepts, all based on play.

Symbolic Play

Functional play is followed developmentally by the onset of a second stage of play, which Piaget refers to as *symbolic play.* In most children about 18 months old, we see the beginning of pretense. That is, we see actions take place out of the context in which they normally take place. We begin to see children at this age who will pick up an empty cup, bring it to their lips, and tip the empty cup in their hands as if to drink. We might also see toddlers take a blanket or towel, pull it over their chins, close their eyes, and pretend to sleep. All advances in symbolic play are characterized by a transformation of signifiers; an understanding of experience from the world becomes translated into actions or depictions by the child.

During the symbolic play stage, an observer might see one of two types of activity develop. One type of activity is *dramatic* or *pretend play.* Pretend play tends to develop through phases beginning with simple actions toward oneself, such as when a child brings an empty cup to her lips and pretends to drink. Later, the child will be able to use objects that do not look like what they are supposed to be, as when a child uses a leaf or a shell to represent a cup from which he may pretend to drink. Eventually children will develop a fuller understanding of the actions they have encountered through their physical exploration of the world. Included in those understandings are sequences of scripted play activities (Bretherton, 1989; Nelson, 1986), in which young children begin by pretending to be their mother or father, or pretending to be Superman or some other character whom they have either witnessed, heard about, or read about. This kind of pretend symbolic play will continue at least until children are seven or eight or, possibly, nine years of age.

A second kind of symbolic play typically seen during the preschool years is *construction play.* Using different materials, children construct objects to represent or depict what they are thinking about. Through their physical manipulation of materials, children develop and elaborate different symbols; mental images are transformed into physical images on which children reflect even further. We see this kind of symbolic play in young children's drawings, as they acquire the knowledge to depict human figures and human settings in their drawings.

Construction play is also manifest in the way children put together different objects such as building blocks, piles of sand, or cushions on the sofa. During construction play, children create symbols by constructing increasingly complex configurations of what they have encountered in real life (Reifel, 1984; Reifel & Greenfield, 1982, 1983). When they build with building blocks, they create houses or other settings. As they mature they will include more parts and details in their settings; as they reach the age of four or five, they begin to use their own constructed play settings as settings for dramatic play. For example, they might begin by building a house out of blocks and then pretend that it is their own house; they will start pretending to be the moms, dads, and other adults with whom they have had interactions in that house. Similarly, they might create a farm or a zoo out of building blocks and make building blocks represent their understanding of barnyards or corrals; they then might pretend to be the farmer or zookeeper who works in those barnyards and corrals (Reifel & Yeatman, 1991). Symbolic play comes together in a form both of construction and dramatic play. Symbolic play continues to be a dominant type of play for young children until they are about age six or seven.

Rule-Based Games

We see many children at about age five or six enter what Piaget (1962) describes as the third stage of play, the play stage of *games with rules.* Games with rules are physical activities children engage in with others, during which their behavior is constrained not only by the physical acts they are doing but also by predetermined rules. When a child plays a game of tag, he or she must learn and respond to the person who is "it" and know that there are rules involved in the game. We know that the person who is "it" chases the others, and all the others must run from the person who is "it". Playing cards, duck-duck-goose, and board games are all different games which take place only with other people. Learning to interact with others is an important by-product of such play. Since the 1980s, we are seeing an increase in children's involvement with games using computers. Games with rules also develop, as all types of play do, through different stages as children acquire more knowledge of the rules, more knowledge about how to interact with others, and also learn the importance of game strategy.

Piaget's three stages of play give us a broad framework for an understanding of children's physical engagement with their environments. It shows how children acquire different cognitive understandings, not only about the environment, but about how people are expected to behave in different environments. Play from Piaget's point of view is seen as an increasingly complex internal structuring of a child's world, and his theory allows us to think about play as a cognitive activity.

Sociocultural Aspects of Developmental Play

Another developmental theorist who gives us many ideas about the significance of play for children's cognitive and social development is Vygotsky (1978). Working concurrently with Piaget, Vygotsky posited play as the process through which children begin to acquire socially construed symbols. That is, materials that children play with and the games that they play allow them to develop a number of different meanings that have significance within the culture in which they are growing. For example, in many societies little girls are given dolls in order to learn more about human relationships and caring; little boys are more likely in Western society to be given cars and trucks to learn about transportation and commerce. We can see that the materials that children act on physically provide them with understandings about what the possible expectations are going to be for them in their society and what it is they are supposed to do and who they are supposed to become in society. From Vygotsky's point of view materials or playthings are very important, because they allow the child to go from physical action on objects to meaning. Manipulating playthings, considered as pivots for meanings, allows the child to go from action alone (i.e., being physical with objects) to developing knowledge about the meanings associated with those actions and objects. A child given a baby book to manipulate will begin to turn pages and pretend to read long before understanding what books are for as well as all that we do with books. From both Piaget's and Vygotsky's points of view, physical action provides a very important basis from which children begin to acquire understandings about who they are, what their society is, and what different symbol systems function within their society.

The works of Piaget, Vygotsky, Garvey ([1977, 1990], who addresses specifically the language and signals of play), and a number of other theorists give ways of understanding what it means to experience the environment, how we make sense of the environment, and how play is an important part of translating our experiences into understanding. The research we have been doing at the University of Texas as well as research at other universities has revealed a great deal about the significance of the materials and people that children physically encounter as they are growing up.

Building on these theoretical bases, let us review some of the research on children's play at home as well as children's play in preschools. We will see how the early experiences of children provide them with a basis for understanding different kinds of literacy and for appreciating the kinds of literacy experiences that educators provide in preschool and school-age years. I will begin by looking at a number of studies of play in the home to see how children's home experiences might shape their earliest appreciation of books, language, and stories.

Literacy Play at Home

We have known for some time that young children who are exposed to books from an early age tend to have an advantage when it comes time to learn to read in schools (Clark, 1984; Durkin, 1966; Leichter, 1984; Morrow & Paratore, 1993). We know that having books and magazines around the home as well as seeing adults participate in reading activities provides not only ideas about the importance of literacy, but also the motivation to participate in other experiences with books.

Recent research on home influences on early literacy demonstrates a full range of possible home influences that contribute to young children's eagerness and readiness to work with books and to learn to read. Roser and her colleagues (Roser, Hoffman, Kastler & Sharp, in press) have interviewed parents to see their perspective on what they do and on what their children do in order to prepare them to be learners who benefit from reading instruction. She and her colleagues have found that providing children with opportunities to interact with literacy related materials appears to be something that parents remember about their children's preschool experience. Parents who do provide support and encouragement for those experiences often have children who are actively involved with books and with the reading process when they enter school.

What is the source of that support and encouragement? Various studies conducted within homes have found a full range of school-related abilities that appear to be nurtured through children's play at home. Some of the research that I have done with my graduate student, June Yeatman, has articulated a variety of preliteracy play activities that children choose to participate in (Yeatman & Reifel, 1992). When older

and younger children play together, since older children usually know more, younger children tend to learn from them
through the process of play. These home-based play experiences provide valuable bases for literacy that operate on a
number of levels. We found that preschool play of sisters, as
documented through an ethnographic study in their home,
tends to include activities such as learning to spell words,
learning the meanings of words, learning the written expression of words, as well as learning the components of storytelling (Yeatman & Reifel, 1992). All of these activities emerge in
the process of play.

Other researchers of preschool children's play have discovered a full range of play opportunities that seem to stimulate children's growing awareness of story, story components,
character, and knowledge about language that is seen as critical for entry into literacy (e.g., Heath, 1983). For example,
Catherine Garvey's (1977, 1990) work with preschool children has found that in the process of play children acquire the
ability to use metacommunicative statements. They make
statements about language that indicate a growing awareness
of different functions that language can serve. Children learn
that they can communicate, and they learn that they can
comment on their communications. It appears that a variety
of children's play activities involving physical engagement
with materials and playmates appears to provide critical bases
for children's understanding of language and literacy, as well
as promoting an interest in literacy.

We can see, especially through observational studies, how
particular play objects such as books, papers, pencils, paints,
and other creative materials may well serve as pivots, in Vygotsky's sense, that allow children to go from physical action
to meanings that are relevant for involvement with literacy
and books. These variables become more salient in studies
done in early childhood classrooms.

Play in the Classroom

A wide variety of studies has addressed the issue of interrela-
tionship of early childhood play to classroom learning. Obser-

vational studies of children in preschool and primary classrooms as well as experimental studies of children in preschool and kindergarten classrooms have identified a number of variables that seem to be relevant to young children's increasing awareness of and facility with written language and literacy.

Play with Materials

An extensive observational study conducted by Miller, Fernie, and Kantor (1992) at Ohio State University discovered a wide range of social and material conditions that appear relevant to understanding children's acquisition of literacy. Over the course of three academic quarters, these researchers observed preschool children during their classroom free-play interactions. These free-play interactions allowed children to be exposed not only to oral language, but increasingly to written language as well as other text from which they appeared to learn more about words, writing, and books. Strategic efforts by teachers to include appropriate objects that allow children to go from action to idea, to verbal expression of that idea, to verbal label of that idea, aid children in becoming increasingly conscious participants in literacy experiences.

For example, at the art table children physically manipulated materials that had been made available for art. One day the teacher put large sheets of paper, paint, and glitter on the art table in order for children to create play-relevant capes; the capes might be used for pretending to be Superman or some other character. Numerous children were attracted to the activity that included creating a glittered insignia on the cape. Many children on their own initiative chose to include their own names to identify their capes, while some chose to create insignia based on their own names. Writing one's name went from a classroom organizational event (for identifying whose art is whose) to a decorative part of the art project. Literacy activities became part of the focus of play, something to play with, rather than being simply a labeling activity.

At the same art table on another day, a balance scale activity with alphabet noodles was available for play. Rather than serving as bulk that could be measured, the noodles themselves became the primary interest for a group of playmates. Seeing the noodles triggered the "ABC Song" for one

time 4 exploration

girl, while another decided to find the letters to spell her own name. The teacher tried to re-direct the children toward the measuring activity, but their interest in using the noodles to create visible language preoccupied them. The meaning of the materials for playing with language was an undeniable draw for the children.

Another kind of play in a different part of the preschool playroom was a context for a range of literacy play. In the block corner, a group of boys typically dominated play. Boys used literacy during block play to create signs, lists or notes, and journal writing (Miller et al., 1992). For example, notes might be used to direct or control play, as when a "Don't sit in our spaceship" sign was prepared to keep others from a play construction. Other signs served as labels for block constructions (e.g., "Transformers"). Dramatic narratives or journals on children's construction-related scenarios were dictated to an adult. All of these uses of literacy related to play functioned to control or direct play, to engage others in play, or to enhance play (Miller et al., 1992, pp. 114–115).

In all of these examples, literacy was intrinsically and naturally related to children's chosen play activities, at times in spite of adults' intended plans. As they played, children came to experience various semantic relationships of language: how literacy functions (e.g., to label,), or how literacy serves an end (e.g., to protect play objects or to keep others away). They also learned more about authorship (who creates a message) and about technical control of literacy (how to form letters). Miller and her colleagues found that children played in a manner that allowed children to make sense "of and through written language." (Goodman, 1986, p. 6). In all cases, literacy makes sense for children because it occurs in the meaningful context of play. Children either initiated the use of print or responded to teacher initiatives that they do so. Research found numerous examples of spontaneously occurring play and literacy.

Literacy Play and the Preschool Classroom Environment

Experimental studies done with preschool children have demonstrated how teachers' efforts to include more book and literacy-related activity tend to increase children's play with regard to those materials and also with regard to the use of language.

Christie (in press) looks at the physical environment of the preschool classroom as a source for literacy play. His review of experimental studies links theoretical descriptions of symbolic play with systematic comparisons of different classroom features. For his perspective on play, Christie draws on Piaget (1962) and Vygotsky (1978), as described above; symbolic pretense is seen as one way of fostering development and learning. His perspective on literacy builds on notions of emergent literacy (Goodman, 1986; Teale, 1987); early home and play experiences have a significant influence on the language, sense-making, and print involvement that are a foundation for literacy. A number of studies support Christie's formulation.

Among the studies that make these ideas salient are a number of experimental manipulations of play environments. The basic paradigm of these studies involves observing children at play in typical classroom settings (i.e., dress-up corner, play kitchen, block center) and observing play in settings that have been altered in subtle ways. For example, Hall, May, Moores, Shearer, and Williams (1987) added pens, pencils, paper, and note pads to a house play center, and telephone books, catalogs, diaries, and stationery to another play center. Christie & Enz (1992) created a whole series of play centers, such as a post office (with pencils, pens, markers, stationery, envelopes, stamps, mail box, address labels, and relevant wall signs) and a library (with pencils, books, shelf labels for books, wall signs, library cards, and check-out cards for books). The question is, what effect do these play materials have on children's play, language, and literacy? In homemaking areas, secretarial areas, or other play areas of the classroom it has been found that including these objects increases the rate at which children include literacy-related play in their more general dramatic play.

What is striking about the studies Christie reviews is the degree to which play materials, and in some instances adult support of play, increase the degree to which children pretend to read and write. Having literacy materials in a classroom leads to children playing with them. In some cases it has been found that such play leads to increased knowledge of some functions of writing (Vukelich, 1991). For many children, classroom play with literacy appears to be an important step in becoming literate. Having literacy materials in the play environment is critical to that step.

A range of research on play and environments (home and school) reveals the significance of materials. Having contact with literacy-related materials, like pens, paper, and books, stimulates dramatic play in a manner that is still being explored, but appears to have great promise for success. Equally suggestive is the research on social play and literacy.

Social Play Foundations for Literacy

A third strand of research dealing with early literacy and play has been conducted by Ann Dyson. She has conducted extensive observational studies of young children's acquisition of literacy, including writing and related reading abilities. Through observations of kindergarteners, first and second graders, and older children, Dyson has been able to document an array of developmental phases for literacy. Children eventually acquire the ability to translate their ideas into words in written form and to refine those words and ideas. Dyson (1982) has found that much writing begins in the process of symbolic representations that frequently takes the form of younger children drawing pictures. Having the idea of putting what is in your mind on paper in the form of pictures appears to be one important way children can start to realize that they have ideas and that those ideas can be documented. As they progress, children will begin to add written words to their pictures. Children come to understand that not only do their ideas have symbolic form, but their ideas have written form and that they can shape that written form through the process of dictation and editing. Several typical social relationships appear to help children shape their creations.

With primary grade children, Dyson (in press) has shown how social relationships are linked to early writing in the primary grades. Children's social play in their neighborhoods and classrooms provides a complex set of foundations for early writing, what Dyson refers to as composition. Acquiring literacy, in the sense of becoming able to shape a language-based communication, is a function of the congruence of a number of meaningful contexts, including social language (i.e., talk), symbolic media (e.g., drawing, dramatic play), cultural customs, and social worlds. Literacy is a way of making sense, and we necessarily make sense through the processes of social interaction. Dyson shows us how a variety of contexts, including play, contribute to this sense making.

Dyson (in press) shows us how neighborhood play and the social cohesion formed thereby relate to narrative and literacy. With remarkable detail and insight, she shows how neighborhood activities, such as religious observances, become part of a pretend narrative; children write about aspects of church services that take a personal, sometimes fantastic, meaning in their own stories ("I flew up to heaven. I flew up to heaven." [Dyson, in press, p. 28]). These narratives form meaningful topics for early composition, including drawing and writing. In the classroom context, pretend narratives are revised through peer response; in order for the narrative to make sense as a composed text, it must make sense to classmates (Dyson, 1989, 1991).

Without neighborhood play experiences that have meaning, children have nothing to make sense of; they need to have something to make sense of, and playmates provide them with the meaningful interactions they need to develop literacy. When they come to the classroom, they want to translate their play-based meanings into compositions, to make sense in a nonplay context. What they do, however, is create a new social play context in the classroom while they compose. As they put down on paper their meanings, they strive to make those meanings sensible to others. They play with each other's texts, revising the meanings for increased clarity. They use play and their social relationships based on play to edit and revise. Caring about friends gets a child involved in text. It ties them to storytelling and provides a foundation for literacy.

Humans appear to have an essential affinity for story (Dyson & Genishi, 1994). We try to organize our thinking and our experience in a way that makes sense. We learn about what makes sense within our communities from stories and other language patterns and from our need to make sense as we communicate. Obviously, experience with literature and other media will contribute to communication. But the most meaningful communications come from the interactions we have with our immediate families and playmates: making sense happens in the immediate contexts in which we function. Those contexts include both classrooms and neighborhoods.

Sociocultural Influences on Children's Storytelling

Social and cultural influences on play and narrative are addressed by Scales & Cook-Gumperz (1993). Building on Paley's (1981) work on children's stories and her work on sex differences (Paley, 1984), they analyze how boys and girls in our society come to create different views of who they are and how their stories should be ordered (Nicolopolou, Scales, & Weintraub, 1984). The preschool girls in their study created standard plots with stable characters; harmonious relationships, especially with stereotypic family characters, were typical of girls' stories. Boys, on the other hand, created more disruptive plot lines with powerful, often frightening characters; violent action, rather than harmony, marked their stories.

Why should there be such dramatic differences between girls' and boys' stories? It seems that these findings can be understood in terms of our sex-differentiated society, wherein gender has all sorts of culturally determined meanings that shape in different ways the development of boys and girls. The toys children are given (as meaningful pivots), the social models they have (in real life, on television, and in books), and the way they are treated differently will cause their stories and other created meanings to follow different paths. Immediate playthings and social contact will have an influence, but sometimes the cultural forces that provide that influence will be far-reaching. In our culture, gender creates a context that shapes play and meaning in significant ways.

Conclusions

Research from the home and from the preschool classroom tends to demonstrate that children will spontaneously engage in physical and social activities that serve as a wellspring for language and literacy experiences. The opportunity to interact with literacy materials seems to stimulate children to use other materials to create meaning. Interaction with others also tends to stimulate that interest as well as to require children to refine their ideas.

Theoretically, most research tends to support formulations derived from Piaget and from Vygotsky. Notions of the importance and of the development of play spring from Piaget's stages. The wealth of research amassed on children's playful manipulation of symbols and construction of knowledge suggests that active involvement with stimulating environments provides a critical developmental foundation for all aspects of mental development, including literacy. Actively doing, with objects and with others, is the key to engaging young children's minds. Ideas from Vygotsky extend that understanding, by showing how social influences shape play and development. Our culture surrounds children with literacy-related symbols, through books, television, and other media. More competent playmates, whether adults or peers, provide a developmental pull to learn more, for all sorts of reasons; sometimes we want to be more competent in order to communicate with those we care for, and sometimes we want to be more competent just to be more competent. In either case, other people serve as our supportive and challenging listeners.

Building on notions of symbolic play and the social shaping of play, we (Reifel & Yeatman, 1991, 1993; Yeatman & Reifel, 1992) have been attempting to describe how children use social pivots as well as physical pivots for creating meaning. Drawing on Vygotsky's (1978) sociocultural theory of development and Bateson's (1972) theory of play, we are looking at how children establish their play frames and create meaning through play. This includes meaningful literacy, as I described above. It seems that play serves the pull of development by means of the physical objects we see as part of our (culturally determined) play environment, by providing a way to create meaning symbolically, and also through the many social interactions we maintain. Our physical actions in play allow us to begin to make meaning.

With regards to early literacy, it seems that playing in environments where language and story are ever-present allows us to make better sense of language and story. Hearing stories (a social activity) gives us something to play about. Playing (frequently a social activity) allows us to create stories. Playing socially (with friends for whom we care) forces us to make ourselves more clear and to refine our stories. Play serves to motivate and to further our earliest efforts to create meaning. These creative efforts blossom in our later involvement with literacy, as children write and as they become interested in fiction.

It seems reasonable and important to link play with literacy for a number of reasons. First, as the research shows, play appears to provide a symbolic foundation for imagining and creating text. Second, play provides the social relationships that allow text and story to develop and become more clear. But equally important is the idea that play provides us with a sense of control and ownership. Through play we learn our interests and strengths. We learn what we like and what pleases us. We learn how to take those interests and follow up on them, to imagine them and to give them life in our imaginations. Play may be one root of our adult involvement with pleasure reading.

This review of research on play and early development has a great deal to say about the importance of books and libraries for young children. Providing children at the earliest ages with appropriate books would seem to be consistent with Vygotsky and Piaget; infants can manipulate and chew on cloth books, toddlers can flip the pages of cardboard picture books, and older preschoolers can begin to explore the picture-text associations in storybooks. In all cases, books become developmentally appropriate (NAEYC, 1986a, 1986b; Bredekamp & Rosegrant, 1992), meaningful materials that can form a stable presence in young children's experiences. Going to the library should be an extension of those experiences. Having playful, welcoming environments where children can explore and imagine with books would seem to be a sensible way to help socialize children into the world of books and literacy. The literature on play has implications for how children's library environments might be arranged to meet their developing interests and needs.

We all are interested in promoting a citizenry of thoughtful, creative individuals. It seems to me that libraries and literacy go together in a manner similar to schools and literacy; both will contribute to our access to and comfort with literacy. This is particularly true in the preschool years, when school and peers are less of a dominant force in children's lives. The early years may be a ripe time to get children hooked on books and libraries, to make libraries a meaningful and necessary part of children's lives. If young children feel at home in the library, they will continue to treat it as an important part of their lives. Perhaps by helping children play appropriately in libraries, we can help them develop a library habit. With such a habit, they might learn to think, create, and eventually solve some of our society's problems.

Works Cited

Bateson, G. (1972). *Steps to an ecology of mind.* New York: Ballantine Books.

Bredekamp, S., & Rosegrant, T. (1992). *Reaching potentials: Appropriate curriculum and assessment for young children* (Vol. 1). Washington, DC: National Association for the Education of Young Children.

Bretherton, I. (1989). Pretense: The form and function of make-believe play. *Developmental Review, 9,* 383–401.

Christie, J. F. (in press). Literacy play interventions: A review of empirical research. In S. Reifel (Ed.), *Advances in early education and day care (Vol. 6): Topics in Early Literacy, Teacher Preparation, and International Perspectives on Early Care.* Greenwich, CT: JAI Press.

Christie, J. F., & Enz, B. (1992). The effects of literacy play interventions on preschoolers' play patterns and literacy development. *Early Education and Development, 3,* 205–220.

Clark, M. M. (1984). Literacy at home and at school: Insights from a study of young fluent readers. In H. Goelman, A. Oberg, & F. Smith (Eds.), *Awakening to literacy* (pp. 122–130). Exeter, NH: Heinemann.

Durkin, D. (1966). *Children who read early.* New York: Teachers College Press.

Dyson, A. H. (1982). Reading, writing, and language: Young children solving the written language puzzle. *Language Arts, 59,* 829–839.

Dyson, A. H. (1989). *Multiple worlds of child writers: Friends learning to write.* New York: Teachers College Press.

Dyson, A. H. (1991). The roots of literacy development: Play, pictures, and peers. In B. Scales, M. Almy, A. Nicolopoulou, & S. Ervin-Tripp (Eds.), *Play and the social context of development in early care and education* (pp. 98–116). New York: Teachers College Press.

Dyson, A. H. (in press). Framing child texts with child worlds: The social use of oral and written narratives. In S. Reifel (Ed.), *Advances in early education and day care (Vol. 6): Topics in Early Literacy, Teacher Preparation, and International Perspectives on Early Care.* Greenwich, CT: JAI Press.

Dyson, A. H., & Genishi, C. (1994). *The need for story: Cultural diversity in classroom and community.* Urbana, IL: National Council of Teachers of English.

Fein, G., & Rivkin, M. (Eds.). (1986). *The young child at play: Reviews of research (Vol. 4).* Washington, DC: NAEYC.

Garvey, C. (1977). Play with language and speech. In S. Ervin-Tripp & C. Mitchell-Kernan (Eds.), *Child discourse* (pp. 27–48). New York: Academic Press.

Garvey, C. (1990). *Play.* Cambridge, MA: Harvard University Press.

Goodman, Y. (1986). Children coming to know literacy. In W. H. Teale & E. Sulzby (Eds.), *Emergent literacy: Writing and reading* (pp. 1–14). Norwood, NJ: Ablex.

Heath, S. B. (1983). *Ways with words: Language, life, and work in communities and classrooms.* New York: Cambridge University Press.

Hall, N., May, E., Moores, J., Shearer, J., & Williams, S. (1987). The literate home-corner. In P. Smith (Ed.), *Parents and teachers together* (pp. 134–144). London: Macmillan.

Leichter, H. J. (1984). Families as environments for literacy. In H. Goelman, A. Oberg, & F. Smith (Eds.), *Awakening to literacy* (pp. 38–50). Exeter, NH: Heinemann.

Miller, S. M., Fernie, D., & Kantor, R. (1992). Distinctive literacies in different preschool play contexts. *Play & Culture, 5* (2), 107–119.

Morrow, L. M. & Paratore, J. (1993). Family literacy: Perspectives and practices. *The Reading Teacher, 47,* 194–200.

National Association for the Education of Young Children. (1986a). Position statement on developmentally appropriate practice in early childhood programs serving children from birth through age 8. *Young Children, 41* (6), 4–19.

NAEYC. (1986b). Position statement on developmentally appropriate practices in programs for 4- and 5-year olds. *Young Children, 41* (6), 20–29.

Nelson, K. (1986). *Event knowledge: Structure and function in development.* Hillsdale, NJ: Erlbaum.

Nicolopoulou, A., Scales, B., & Weintraub, J. (1994). Gender differences and symbolic imagination in the stories of four-year-olds. In A. Dyson & C. Genishi (Eds.), *The need for story: Cultural diversity in classroom and community* (pp. 102–123). Urbana, IL: National Council of Teachers of English.

Paley, V. (1981). *Wally's stories.* Cambridge, MA: Harvard University Press.

Paley, V. (1984). *Boys and girls: Superheroes in the doll corner.* Chicago: University of Chicago Press.

Piaget, J. (1962). *Play, dreams, and imitation in childhood* (C. Gattegno & F. M. Hodgson, Trans.). New York: W. W. Norton. (Original work published 1951)

Reifel, S. (1984). Block construction: Children's developmental landmarks in representation of space. *Young Children, 40*(1), 61–76.

Reifel, S. (1993). From theory to practice: Observing and thinking about children's play. In M. Guddemi & T. Jambor (Eds.), *A right to play* (pp. 124–127). Little Rock, AR: Southern Early Childhood Association.

Reifel, S. & Greenfield, P. M. (1982). Structural development in a symbolic medium: The representational use of block constructions. In G.E. Forman (Ed.), *Action and thought: From sensorimotor schemes to symbolic operations* (pp. 203–233). New York: Academic Press.

Reifel, S. & Greenfield, P. M. (1983). Part-whole relations: Some structural features of children's representational block play. *Child Care Quarterly, 12*(1), 144–151.

Reifel, S. & Yeatman, J. (1991). Action, talk, and thought in block play. In B. Scales, M. Almy, A. Nicolopoulou, & S. Ervin-Tripp (Eds.), *Play and the social context of development in early care and education* (pp. 156–172). New York: Teachers College Press.

Reifel, S. & Yeatman, J. (1993). From category to context: Reconsidering classroom play. *Early Childhood Research Quarterly, 8,* 347–367.

Rubin, K. H., Fein, G. G., & Vandenberg, B. (1983). Play. In E. M. Hetherington (Ed.), *Handbook of child psychology: Vol. 4. Socialization, personality and social development.* New York: Wiley.

Roser, N., Hoffman, J., Kastler, L., & Sharp, C. (in press). What parents tell us about children's emerging literacy. In S. Reifel (Ed.), *Advances in early education and day care (Vol. 6): Topics in early literacy, teacher preparation, and international perspectives on early care.* Greenwich, CT: JAI Press.

Scales, B. & Cook-Gumperz, J. (1993). Gender and play in nursery and preschool: A view from the frontier. In S. Reifel (Ed.), *Advances in early education and day care (Vol. 5): Perspectives on developmentally appropriate practice* (pp. 167–196). Greenwich, CT: JAI Press.

Smith, P. R. (1982). Does play matter? Functional and evolutionary aspects of animal and human play. *The Behavioral and Brain Sciences, 5,* 139–184.

Teale, W. H. (1987). Emergent literacy: Reading and writing development in early childhood. In J. E. Readence & R. S. Baldwin (Eds.), *Research in literacy: Merging perspectives.* Thirty-sixth yearbook of the National Reading Conference (pp. 45–74). Rochester, NY: National Reading Conference.

Vukelich, C. (1991). Materials and modeling: Promoting literacy during play. In J. F. Christie (Ed.), *Play and early literacy development* (pp. 215–231). Albany, NY: State University of New York Press.

Vygotsky, L. S. (1978). *Mind in society: The development of higher psychological processes.* Cambridge, MA: Harvard University Press.

Yeatman, J. & Reifel, S. (1992). Sibling play and learning. *Play & Culture, 5*(2), 141–158.

CHAPTER 3

Children's Socioemotional Development
Implications for School Readiness

ALICE STERLING HONIG

Intellectual abilities of children and their potential for school readiness and early learning can only be optimized when their emotional security, self-esteem, and social supports from intimate others are nurtured along with their cognitive competence. Children learn best if the emotional climate in which they grow lets them feel good about themselves as learners and as kind and cooperative persons, rather than as frightened, defensive, or angry individuals. Parents, childcare workers, and teachers have always been considered primary persons in the vanguard of providing early positive nurturing.

Today, many children live in distressed, harried, and sometimes dysfunctional family situations. The need for positive adult supports in their lives is acute. Libraries are professionally well placed, both in familiar civic locales and in public confidence, to become service outposts for nurturing families

ALICE STERLING HONIG is professor in the Department of Child and Family Studies, College of Human Development at Syracuse University, where she teaches courses in parenting, theories and applications for child development, preschool models and programs, and prosocial and moral development. Her books include *Parent Involvement in Early Childhood Education* and (with D. S. Wittmer) *Prosocial Development in Children: Caring, Sharing, and Cooperation.*

and children's positive development. Librarians can well appreciate the fundamental importance of emotional development as the basis for *fueling* children's motivation to read and learn. Knowledge about children's emotional development will boost professional adults' abilities to nurture children's motivation to succeed in school.

. To expand horizons of service requires new *awareness,* in particular the knowledge of children's socioemotional development, and new *skills,* ways to reach out from the base of the professional facility to families who may not make language and literacy learning a high priority. Many children cease to use libraries for pleasure reading or for finding out more about the world after they graduate from public school. The ability to motivate a lifelong demand for and use of library facilities so that youngsters can continue a lifetime of learning requires new conceptualizations of the role of librarian and new sensitivity to child and family development. Librarians who work to boost school readiness through sensitive engagement with children and with families ensure that future generations will more surely revere and become engaged with literature in those repositories of knowledge and pleasure we call libraries.

Socioemotional Development

How do children become emotionally mature, motivated learners, positive in their interactions with peers, parents, and other adult mentors, such as teachers and librarians?

This chapter will discuss the beginnings of prosocial and aggressive emotional systems, including the biological bases for the development of temperament styles and personal emotional patterns, and the family functioning that enhances secure emotional attachment and the building of positive self-esteem. Sex differences in the trajectory of socioemotional development will be noted and the relation of young children's competence in sociodramatic play to their cognitive and language competence. The effects of television and of varied cultural and ethnic milieux on differences in socioemotional styles and interactions will be discussed.

Emotional development involves the organization of internal and interactional processes that regulate the expression of communication. Babies a few weeks old are able to smile with pleasure when a nurturing adult smiles and coos to them and caresses them tenderly. They cry with fierce despair when hungry or roughly handled. So sensitive are infants to maternal emotions that infants brought up by depressed, sad mothers will, by three months, act depressed and have different levels of blood chemicals from babies with normal mothers. Despite the early appearance of arms flailing in anger or a crooked grin of pleasure, psychologists believe that "true emotions are not possible until the baby has a sense of self at about nine months" (Sroufe, 1979). Babies learn emotional responses socially by "referencing" the faces and body postures of their caregivers. A baby reaching toward a forbidden object, such as a breakable vase on a coffee table, looks up and sees her caregiver's tense and angry face; she freezes, looks troubled, and turns away.

Sophisticated emotional learning requires years of maturing (Honig 1994b). The basic emotional categories that toddlers learn are *mad, sad,* and *glad.*

> Dana was asleep for her nap when her familiar caregiver (with whom she had a warm relationship) arrived, and her parents then left on an errand. When Dana awoke and saw that her parents were not there, she began to cry. The caregiver soothed her, cuddled her, and remarked, "You are feeling so sad and so mad. You wanted papa and mama to be here when you woke up. You wish they were here right now. You are feeling so mad and so sad!" Having acknowledged the toddler's feelings with "active listening" (Gordon, 1970), Anne went on to change Dana's diaper, read her a story, and play games with her. A few hours later, when her parents opened the front door, Dana ran over to greet them while calling out, "Me so mad and me so sad!" to explain about how she had felt.

Adult use of labels to denote emotions is very important. The two-year-old who is running merrily with a wide grin toward the tricycle just vacated by a peer needs to be validated:

"Maija, you are feeling so happy. The tricycle is free now. You were waiting so patiently because you really want to ride on the trike. You are smiling and feeling so happy." More subtle emotions that youngsters feel, such as chagrin, jealousy, or longing may take years to understand cognitively, even though the behavioral expressions of such emotions can be seen in toddlers.

Singing has deep emotional healing power. It helps children to become calm and it reassures them when they are emotionally upset. Lullabies and chants are emotional restoratives.

> Miss Alice was a new caregiver whom Natalie Bess did not yet know well. When the 19-month-old awoke from her nap, she started to cry forlornly. As Miss Alice drew near the crib, Natalie Bess looked at her from lowered lids and seemed ready to bawl even louder. The caregiver began to sing softly on just a few simple tones. "Natalie Bess is waking up from her nap time. Natalie is waking up. Natalie is getting up from her sleepy-sleep time. Guess who is waking up now. Natalie Bess is finishing her nap. Soon we will change her diaper. Soon she will have some milk. Natalie Bess had a good nap time. Now it is time to wake up."

This simple chant with hypnotic repetitions reassured the baby that her caregiver cared about her personally and would comfort her and stay tuned in to her readiness to wake fully and be prepared for childcare. Such sensitivity to a child's tempo increases chances that a baby will retain *or* regain emotional control over distress. Parents need books to browse with simple chants and melodies, finger plays, and lullabies, as well as recorded songs on cassettes.

Learning complexities about emotions

Understanding that two different emotions can be felt together, even when they are conflicting, is a very difficult concept for preschoolers to grasp. The toddler who wants to poke fingers in a wall plug but wants also to please the parent who has forbidden this exciting activity may stretch out her fingers, then pull them back murmuring, "No, no, no. Bad girl."

Wanting to be cooperative and yet longing for the forbidden are opposing emotions that wrestle in the souls of toddlers as well as adults. Parents need to understand how powerful the emotions of young children are (Kuebli, 1994; Lewis & Saarni, 1985). Rather than ridicule or anger, young ones need adult understanding and adult support for their budding attempts to control immature and inappropriate emotional outbursts or temper tantrums.

Adults particularly need to point out how important it is for children to coordinate their emotional wants and wishes with others. For example, a child may fight with a best friend because the friend does not want to play the same game as the child. Parents need to teach children that others may have different emotions and wants. Friends need to take turns or figure out ways each one of them can get their wishes some of the time and the other person's wishes some of the time. This "win-win" (Gordon, 1970) conceptualization of negotiating solutions to disagreements must be carefully explained over and over to small children, who often see the world in simplistic bad or good terms. By preschool, children themselves can be encouraged to create alternative solutions as well as conceptualize the consequences of each solution they propose for their socioemotional conflicts.

Piagetian theory suggests that decentering and taking the emotional or cognitive viewpoint of the other is difficult for the preoperational child before six or seven years of age. For full emotional comprehension of the nuances of other's feelings this may be true. But research has clearly shown that even toddlers can understand the feelings of a distressed baby and return a cookie that fell from the hand of the baby in the high chair. Toddlers can recognize that a parent coming home from work with a pounding headache needs rest and quiet time for a while before starting to play with the child. Some toddlers will even cover a tired parent with their own blankie. "Baby altruists" are not just born that way. Research, based on analysis of parental tape recordings of toddler and family responses to emotionally salient and distressful events, revealed that parents of "baby altruists" had been consistent *positive role models* (Pines, 1979). They provided tender caressing and reassurance when an infant was feeling hurt or upset. They also firmly and vigorously discouraged and would not accept toddler use of aggressive actions for solving any social distress/problem (such as jealous anger at the new baby or wanting to snatch a playmate's toy).

Temperament

One important aspect of emotional development is the pervasive influence of temperament. Temperament refers to "individual differences in the intensive and temporal parameters of behavioral expressions of emotionality and arousal, especially as these differences influence the organization of intrapersonal and interpersonal processes" (Campos, Barrett, Lamb, Goldsmith, & Stenberg, 1984, p. 832). Nine different temperamental attributes have been discerned:

1. rhythm
2. activity level
3. approach vs. avoidance
4. adaptability
5. mood
6. persistence/attention span
7. threshold for distress
8. response intensity
9. distractability.

Some babies are more *rhythmic* in their bodily functioning. They void or nurse on a regular schedule. Other babies sleep or feed irregularly. Parents sometimes feel more irritable and tense toward babies who are low in rhythmicity, especially if baby wakes many times a night and parents cannot nap during the day. But the biological basis for temperament attributes means that babies need to be understood rather than blamed by parents. Some babies are highly wiggly and *active*. As toddlers, they are on the run so much that often a parent cannot get them to lie still for a diapering. Parents may have to change a diaper midcourse, as it were, while the toddler is busy waddling down a hallway. Other babies are more calm and peaceable. They can stay put, for example, if given a shovel and pail and set down to play in a sand pile. Some babies approach new people and new experiences with zest. Others withdraw fearfully or suspiciously. They need slow introductions to a teaspoon of new food or to a new caregiver. Rather than avoid the new, some tots welcome and thrive on new experiences. They are *adaptable* and parents may be able to take such children more easily on trips or to visit strangers. *Mood* differs among babies. Some children are more solemn. Others are more cheerful and smile more readily. Some children are highly *persistent.* They can work long at a puzzle or listen to a very long story. Others have a more fleeting attention span and need to be lured into lengthy attention to school or home tasks.

Some children have a high tolerance for distress. While practicing walking, for example, when they sprawl hard on the floor, they pick themselves up without fuss and keep on trying. Their *threshold for distress* is high. Other children react to pain or fright very easily. Children also differ in the *intensity of their response* to fear and pain. Some hungry babies can tolerate a little wait until they are nursed. Other children react to an empty tummy with intense crying, or with screaming terror if faced with a fearful stimulus, such as a barking dog or a scary wind-up toy. More *distractible* children may be easily comforted when upset. Indeed, some are so distractible that they need a quiet environment if they are to settle into sleep and need special quiet places to do their homework. Others are not easily distracted from their pursuits and may have to be called to supper many times when they are deeply absorbed in play or reading a book.

From long-term studies of children with these nine temperament traits, Thomas and Chess (1977) derived three predominant temperament types:

1. the slow-to-warm-up or fearful child (about 15 percent of the sample), characterized by low-key mood, withdrawal, low adaptability, and low intensity;
2. the difficult child (about 10 percent), sometimes called feisty, with low adaptability, low rhythmicity, irritable mood, low threshold of tolerance for distress, and high intensity of response to fear or displeasure;
3. the easy child (40 percent) with high soothability and adaptability, positive mood, high rhythmicity and approachability, and low intensity of response to distress.

Most parents are unaware of the powerful impact of their care on the socioemotional growth of their babies. Some see children as deliberately screaming or aggressing in order to aggravate the adults. Parents need help in understanding temperament attributes and learning to deal tolerantly and calmly with each temperament style. They may need to learn more soothing techniques, such as swaddling an infant, or humming soothing melodies to a tense child, or redirecting and refocusing a child engaged in unacceptable behaviors (Caldwell, 1977; Honig, 1985b).

Some children require more effort for adults to rear. When a difficult child, with disrupted sleep patterns that already exhaust the parent, screams angrily and hits out at a younger sibling who has toddled over happily to add a block to the child's building, an overstressed parent may want to label that child as "bad" and even punish the child severely. Sometimes a cycle of coercive, inappropriate interactions in that family then results, with frequent outbursts and sequences of anger, punitiveness, defiance, and emotionally maladaptive inter-changes (Patterson, 1984). The videotape "Flexible, Fearful, and Feisty" (California State Department of Education, 1990) is a fine teaching tool for deciphering temperament. Parents viewing the video learn to recognize and more effectively manage the particular temperament style of each of their chil-dren. Calm approaches and firm cheerful guiding plus extra patience and adept preventive maneuvers in childrearing are demonstrated in this video.

Parenting Style: Relation to Child Socioemotional Development

Many parents were themselves reared by punitive or authori-tarian methods. They are often bewildered and dismiss as "weak" those who propose that gentler, verbal reasoning (*inductive*) methods of childrearing will result in more coop-erative, more self-disciplined children (Damon, 1988; Eisen-berg & Mussen, 1989). Yet an awesome volume of research attests to the fact that *authoritarian* ("Do as I say because I am your parent!") and, especially, physically punitive parenting produces more bullies and angry defiant children. Working in the prison system in Bridgeport, Welsh (1976) found that the severity of convicted juvenile delinquency acts was directly proportional to the severity of physical punishment used by parents in raising that delinquent youngster. On the other hand, *permissive* parenting styles with vague or inconsistent parental guidance produce more selfish, less self-disciplined children.

In contrast, the *authoritative* style, which features lots of love, high expectations and demands for moral maturity, clear family rules and reasons for the rules, positive personal engagement with the child, and unconditional loving commitment to the child's well-being, produces more cooperative, more self-disciplined children who are easier to live with both at home and in the classroom. Baumrind's (1977) essay on her longitudinal findings about the importance of parenting style for producing more cooperative, self-actualized, reasonable children needs to be made available freely for parents to read and discuss in workshops on positive discipline.

Trust Building and Attachment: Keys to Positive Parenting

Several theorists have given us great insight into emotional development during the early years.

Margaret Mahler

Mahler, a psychoanalyst who studied mother-infant interactions in exquisite detail over many years, discovered the developmental stages through which a dependent child struggles to separate emotionally from the parent and become an independent individual. At about five or six months, the infant who has been concentrating on *inner* signals of a hungry tummy, a painful gas bubble, or a skin hunger for close cuddling, now has learned to trust parental responsive nurturing to such an extent that the baby can turn *outward* emotionally. With bright eyes and happy interest, the baby sits in

papa's or mama's arms and greets the world of new people and
events with newly emerging emotional zest. This bright-eyed
alertness is what Mahler called the "hatched look." Later, the
newly locomoting baby pushes off on all four paws to explore
the world, and then gains even greater joy at mastering upright toddling. Secure still in feeling protected and generously
provided for by the parent, the toddler experiences an intense
joy at mastery of locomotion and of early language. Imagine
the power! Even one word will get an adult to offer a toy or a
cup of juice or a hug. The toddler enjoys this feeling of early
upright mastery of limbs and of language-based communication skills.

Somewhere near the middle of the second year, toddlers
begin to experience a new cognitive awareness that impels
strong emotional changes. Toddlers begin to realize that a parent will not come or be there for every whim. Food or toys will
not be forthcoming immediately when demanded. The con-
flicted toddler, wanting the blissful reassurance of earlier
indulgences and yet striving mightily to grow toward more
mature independence, now *seesaws* between overdemanding
behavior and development toward more adaptable autonomy.
She learns to accept alternate childcare for part of a day, or to
respond to new demands for mature food eating with utensils,
for example. During this emotionally stressful period, a toddler shadows a parent, or pesters a reading parent by piling
toys in her lap and insisting she read his book to him, or
announces "No" defiantly when asked to get into the bath, or
out of it.

To this emotionally "grey, crashing down period" (Honig,
1993b), Mahler gave the technical term *rapprochement period* (Kaplan, 1978). This is a fateful time for infant mental
health and positive emotional development. Some parents
resent this strangely uncooperative, grumpy toddler who so
defies them. Parents of toddlers need library materials to help
them understand this special period and show them how to
survive with self-esteem of both parent and toddler intact.
Parents who understand the emotional struggle going on in
the toddler may be more empathic and more patient during
this very difficult period, coming as it does on the heels of a
honeymoon period of baby joy and satisfaction.

Parents also need the hopeful information that at the end of the toddler period, preschoolers who have had their emotional needs understood and their emerging sense of self-esteem sustained, will emerge with emotional *constancy,* an ability to reconcile bad and good aspects of persons. With constancy, children have the ability to reconcile imperious needs for "right away" with needs to "wait a while." A child learns that the "bad papa" who will not let her have two ice creams just before dinner is also the "good papa" who holds her on his shoulders lovingly during a visit to the zoo and who snuggles her for a leisurely bedtime story at night. With the emergence of constancy, children begin to reconcile opposite emotions. The well-nurtured preschool child has internalized the goodness of a loving parent and can manage to handle some griefs, fears, displeasures, and losses without feeling the inner terror of abandonment, emptiness, and unlovedness. This inner feeling of emotional abandonment is pernicious. It pervades the consumer culture of some adults. People feel they can "fill up" with material goods and emotional "thrills" such as drug highs, when what they really lost out on in the early years was an inner fullness with good feelings and an inner certainty of being a child who was lovable and deeply cherished emotionally.

Erik Erikson

Neopsychoanalyst Erikson's dialectical theory of the tug between positive emotional learning and more negative polarities allows parents insights into the struggle children have in moving through dialectical conflicts (Erikson, 1963; Honig, 1993a). Young children must learn to become more trusting than mistrusting; to express willfulness in coordination with others' wills and wishes (difficult as this early learning can be); to become more assertive and take responsible initiatives; to be more creative and venturesome in making social plans; and creative also in playing with peers in ways that permit the development of friendships and the exercising of moral choices in ever more judicious ways. The harsh parent who ridicules and shames a child leaves a lasting legacy of pain, defiance, shame, and rage. Bullies are born in that cauldron of inappropriate parental shaming or hurtful responses to early emotional absurdities so typical of toddlerhood—such as a toddler who stubbornly insists he *"can so"* tie his own shoe-laces, or wear a swimsuit to play out in the snow.

Firmness, patience, understanding of seesawing stages, and, above all, *empathy* with and firm guidance for the young child struggling to become emotionally mature, can help parents understand and provide for the emotional needs of their sometimes exasperating toddlers. Difficult as it is emotionally, parents should never get trapped into negative struggles for power or revenge, even with a toddler who has scribbled on the wall or "made a poop" on the bedcovers. Adults who return hurt for hurt will have children who learn that lesson deeply. In school, these children may act out defiantly until a teacher yells at or punishes them. Children learn only too well, and re-create with chilling intensity and accuracy, inappropriate harsh negative emotional interactions (Wittmer & Honig, 1990).

Attachment theorists

Bowlby, Ainsworth, Sroufe, Main, and others have provided us with a wonderful legacy of theoretical and research writings illuminating the powerful relationship between a child's secure early attachment to parents and later positive socioemotional functioning (Honig, 1990; 1993b). Nonverbal, internal working models of emotional relationships are built in from early infancy onward, based on the innumerable acts of responsive caring or harsh indifference; the tuned-in attentiveness or the ridicule, neglect, or shaming; the physically tender cuddling or the rough, scary handling or hitting that a child receives. Thus, each child learns essentially both the role of child *and* the role of punitive or nurturing parent. So powerful are these unconscious learned roles that even parents who hated the way they were mistreated may find themselves reenacting punitive or rejecting interactions.

Adults need to understand their own emotions in the sometimes difficult transitions to parenthood (Belsky, 1994). Mental health specialists who give workshops for parents troubled by the violence of their own angers or resentments

toward little ones provide a deeply important and reward-
ing experience for parents. With professional guidance, the
ghosts from a parent's past can be conjured up and banished.
Although they might have learned raging, ridicule, indifference, or coldness in their own families, parents can slowly
relearn how to nurture, nuzzle, empathize with, respond appropriately, protect, and soothe distressed babies. They can
learn to use humor, firmness, reasoning, and empathic reassurance in rearing emotionally healthy children.

Ainsworth's work reveals that the securely attached infant
is emotionally able to express displeasure at a parent's leaving, and emotionally able to ask for and accept comfort on the
parent's return. Indeed, the securely attached infant can accept reassuring words and smiles on reunion, or accept pats
and hugs when picked up so that he relaxes in a molding way
into the parent's arms. The secure baby can then organize his
emotional strength to go on to play again with toys in a competent manner. In contrast, insecurely attached babies express a variety of emotionally troubled behaviors. On reunion
after separation, avoidantly attached infants ignore the parent
with seeming indifference. They have learned that emotional
reassurance and comfort are not predictably available from
that parent. Ambivalently attached babies ask to be picked up
and comforted on reunion after separation, but then cannot
bodily gather emotional reassurance from the contact. They
squirm to get down or even strike at the parent. Babies with
dazed/disorganized insecure attachments may seem to move
toward asking for bodily comfort on reunion, but then stop,
stare, or turn away.

A parent worried by her or his strong angers or revulsions
can find ways to actualize kindness and caring instead. A
parent can learn where that screaming, hating voice the child
hears actually came from far back in the parent's childhood.
Parents can be helped to banish the searing griefs that in-
vaded their own emotional past, and learn with support how
to respond sensitively and warmly to infant signals of distress,
how to cuddle, coo, and smile tenderly, so that this new baby
can develop a secure rather than insecure attachment.

Prevention of emotional troubles later in life begins in
infancy. Ghosts from their own troubled childhoods do not

have to continue to haunt the lives of new parents (Fraiberg, Shapiro, & Adelson, 1984). Parents need resources to emerge from frozen or hating dark scenarios of their own childhoods. For example, Greenspan & Greenspan's (1985) book *First Feelings* is written in a clear style for parents, encouraging them to create emotional ideas for toddlers. The authors note that "the emotions that most frequently cause a child to regress are separation and loss, aggression and anger, and interest in the body" (p. 245). The authors help parents learn ways to boost young children's ability to separate reality from fantasy and to develop self-esteem.

Emotions and Sex of Child

During the preschool years children begin to play more and more in same-sex groups. Boys play more active, cooperative games, such as building a set of train tracks on which to run toy cars. They may put on paper bag masks with eye slits and soda-bottle caps pasted on as robot facial features as they play outer space games. Little girls may be playing in the doll or dress-up corner. Leaders of play groups try hard to lure males and females into more gender-neutral activities. Indeed, housekeeping corner, water table, playdough, clay, and block area provide wonderful opportunities for boys and girls to share pleasureful play together. Yet strong needs of children to feel that the other sex is somehow the "enemy" may well persist. Some emotional preference for same-sex play groups must be accepted within the larger adult goal of achieving harmonious relationships among all the children in a social group.

Boys and girls are often differentially socialized. Interestingly, boys are more often punished *and* given more positive adult attention. Girls' verbalizations are interrupted more frequently by parents. Fathers are far more disapproving of boys who choose feminine toys or activities than they are of tomboy activities of little girls. The pervasive sex-differentiated gender socialization of children makes it imperative that prosocial messages of caring, helpfulness, kindness, sharing, and cooperation are frequently taught regardless of gender or play proclivities (Honig, 1982b). In society *both* boys and girls need to be brought up to be *agentic* (active initiators) *and competent as well as kind and compassionate.*

Television and Aggression Learning

Research over recent decades has revealed clearly the impact of watching violent television on emotional learning. Eight-year-old children who had watched much television violence were far more likely to be nominated as aggressive by their senior high school classmates ten years later and to have more convictions of drunk driving (Eron, 1982). Children who believed that television characters are "real" rather than imaginary were nominated as more aggressive by their peers. Also, children who had frequently been read fairy tales were less aggressive. Regular viewing of a prosocial TV program, like "Mister Rogers Neighborhood," results in increased tolerance, patience, and friendly play among low-income children (Friedrich & Stein, 1975). Sex role stereotypes and violent interactions are emphasized markedly by children's cartoons.

Television has been called "the plug-in drug." This drug can be used for healing, for nurturing intellectual curiosity, and prosocial development, or it can serve as a powerful potion to desensitize children so that they readily accept violence and aggression. Parents are the gatekeepers of a young child's TV viewing. They need to be informed about the positive values of television and about the more sinister aspects of violent TV watching. Then they can make more enlightened choices for their children.

Sociodramatic Play

Skilled nursery teachers have always known how valuable sociodramatic play can be to help children learn to develop positive friendship interaction patterns as well as to work though fears or scenarios from the home that are causing tension or worry. Particularly useful for professionals is Smilansky & Shefatya's (1990) book *Facilitating Play: A*

Medium for Promoting Cognitive, Socioemotional, and Academic Development in Young Children. Many parents are puzzled about the value of sociodramatic play for early learning. Smilansky & Shefatya point out the intellectual and emotional importance of play. Children concentrate around a given theme; selectively draw on experiences in order to focus on their theme (such as space station play); control their emotions to coordinate with the orderly rubric of an evolving theme; use concentration and also flexibility in carrying out a theme; use friendship ploys in order to involve others; increase sensitivity to peers in order to keep the play moving and developing; and develop respect for the roles that others carry out within the sociodramatic theme. Sociodramatic role play helps children grow toward emotional maturity as they cooperate with others.

Implementation in Libraries

The library is a splendid, sometimes underutilized community resource for boosting effective parenting and thus children's positive socioemotional development. Libraries serve as resource centers for parent education groups and parenting materials. Rugs, easy chairs, bean bag chairs, and a box of sturdy toys in the library can create an inviting area for children as their parents browse and learn more about how children grow and how to tune in empathically in order to cope with the emotional vagaries of toddlers. Additionally, parents should be invited to attend story reading times. As parents watch a skilled librarian model reading to enthralled little ones, they learn how to modulate voice tones and add variety to the way words are used in order to attract children to a love of story time and books.

If parents cannot attend group programs, then libraries can make available easy-to-read, brief articles, such as "The Art of Talking to a Baby" (Honig, 1985a) or "Parent Involvement in the Early Years" (Honig, 1994a). Books that offer suggestions for positive discipline and childrearing are important to display prominently (Briggs, 1975; Crary, 1984; Faber & Mazlish, 1980; Lickona, 1983). Gordon's work (1970) on

Parent Effectiveness Training, which facilitates meaningful and honest communication between parents and children, is especially useful. Many parents become enraged when a toddler spills juice or has a toileting accident and are unaware of the struggles involved in mastering such skills. Display of charts of developmental norms may help parents empathize with and gain insights into the seesawing pathways by which, over time, young children gain inner emotional as well as physical controls.

While parenting book centers in bookstores and in libraries often provide ample resources for middle-class, highly literate parents, additional sensitivity is required to meet the multicultural needs of families who may be of low literacy or bilingual and need easy-to-read parenting materials. *Playtime Learning Games for Young Children* (Honig, 1982a), written at a fifth-grade reading level, encourages parents of young children to use laundry time, grocery shopping, and cooking times as learning opportunities to teach concepts and kindness to children. This book describes teaching tips, such as "matchmaking" the level of teaching to the child's understanding, and "dancing the developmental ladder" as a way to make games and learning interchanges more in tune with the emotional and cognitive needs of the learner.

Outreach programs for child-care providers and centers are as essential as library efforts for parents. Materials for lending to teachers in child-care facilities and kindergartens can implement this cooperation. Video as well as book and kit materials need to be included (Adcock & Segal, 1983; Bellanca, 1991; Bos, 1990; Davis, 1977; Honig & Lally, 1981; Dreikurs, et al., 1990; Gordon, 1974; Kobak, 1979; Shure, 1992; and Smith, 1983). Brief resumes of research and synopses of practical resources are available in Honig & Wittmer's (1993) bibliographic resource guide for enhancing children's prosocial development.

Informational and collaborative networks of librarians and other professionals who serve preschoolers in child care can promote secure emotional growth so that a child grows up deeply confident that he or she is lovable and loved. This emotional foundation supports positive attitudes toward learning and presages with high probability that, with the help of adult mentors, each child will become the kind of learner and reader who will succeed in school, in peer play, and as a cherished family member. Furthering the preparation of very young children for early learning success within a context of positive appreciation of personhood as well as of books can best ensure school readiness.

Proactive library programs whereby librarians *reach-out as well as teach-in with families* can help parents become positively involved with infant and toddler growth toward literacy within a loving, responsive parenting context. Library efforts that support an early passion for language and book reading in infants and very young children will provide a crucial link with preschool educators and families in enhancing school readiness.

· **Works Cited**

Adcock, D., & Segal, M. (1983). *Play together, grow together: A cooperative curriculum for teachers of young children.* White Plains, NY: Mailman Press.

Baumrind, D. (1977). Some thoughts about childrearing. In S. Cohen & T. Comiskey (Eds.), *Child development: Contemporary perspectives.* Itasca, IL: Peacock.

Bellanca, J. (1991). *Building a caring, cooperative classroom: A social skills primer.* Palatine, IL: Skylight Publishing.

Belsky, J., & Kelly, J. (1994). *The transition to parenthood: How a first child changes a marriage.* New York: Delacorte Press.

Bos, B. (1990). *Together we're better: Establishing a coactive learning environment.* Roseville, CA: Turn the Page Press.

Briggs, D. C. (1975). *Your child's self esteem.* New York, NY: Dolphin.

Caldwell, B. M. (1977). Aggression and hostility in young children. *Young Children, 32,* 4–13.

California State Department of Education. (1990). Flexible, fearful and feisty: The different temperaments of infants and toddlers. (Video). *Child Care Video Magazine,* Sacramento, CA: Far West Regional Laboratory and California State Department of Education Program for Infant/toddler Caregivers.

Campos, J. J. , Barrett, K. C., Lamb, M. E., Goldsmith, H. H., Stenberg, C. (1984). Socioemotional development. In M. M. Haith & J. J. Campos (Eds.) *Infancy and developmental psychobiology* (Vol. 2). In P. H. Mussen (Ed.). *Handbook of Child Psychology* (4th ed.) (pp. 783–916).

Crary, E. (1984). *Kids can cooperate: A practical guide to teaching problem solving.* Seattle, WA: Parenting Press.

Damon, W. (1988). *The moral child. Nurturing children's natural moral growth.* New York: Free Press.

Davis, D. E. (1977). *My friends and me.* Circle Pines, MN: American Guidance Service.

Dreikurs, R., Grunwald, B. B., & Pepper, F. C. (1990). *Maintaining sanity in the classroom: Illustrated teaching techniques.* Scranton, PA: Harper-Collins.

Eisenberg, N. & Mussen, P. H. (1989). *The roots of prosocial behavior in children* (2nd ed.). New York: Cambridge University Press.

Erikson, E. (1963). *Childhood and society.* New York: Norton.

Eron, L. D. (1982). Parent-child interaction, television violence and aggression of children. *American Psychologist, 37,* 197–121.

Faber, A., & Mazlish, E. (1980). *How to talk so kids will listen and listen so kids will talk.* New York: Avery Books.

Fraiberg, S., Shapiro, V., & Adelson, E. (1984). Ghosts in the nursery: A psychoanalytic approach to the problems of impaired infant-mother relationships. In L. Fraiberg (Ed.), *Clinical studies in infant mental health* (pp. 100–136). Columbus, OH: Ohio University Press.

Friedrich, L. K., & Stein, A. H. (1975). Prosocial television and young children: The effects of verbal labelling and role-playing on learning and behavior. *Child Development, 46,* 27–38.

Gordon, T. (1970). *Parent effectiveness training.* New York: Wyden.

Gordon, T. (1974). *Teacher effectiveness training for the classroom: How teachers can bring out the best in their students.* New York: Wyden.

Greenspan, S., & Greenspan, N. T. (1985). *First feelings: Milestones in the emotional development of your baby and child.* New York: Penguin.

Honig, A. S. (1982a). *Playtime learning games for young children.* Syracuse, NY: Syracuse University Press.

Honig, A. S. (1982b). Research in review: Prosocial development in children. *Young Children, 37*(5), 51–63.

Honig, A. S. (1985a). The art of talking to a baby. *Working Mother, 8*(3), 72–78.

Honig, A. S. (1985b). Research in review: Cooperation, compliance, and discipline. *Young Children,* Part I, *40*(2), 50–58; Part II, *40*(3), 47–52.

Honig, A. S. (1990). Infant/toddler education: Principles, practices and promises. In C. Seefeldt (Ed.), *Continuing issues in early childhood education* (pp. 61–105). Columbus, OH: Merrill.

Honig, A. S. (1993a). The Eriksonian approach. In J. L. Roopnarine (Ed.), *Approaches to early childhood education* (2nd ed.) (pp. 47–70). New York: Macmillan.

Honig, A. S. (1993b). Mental health for babies: What do theory and research teach us? *Young Children, 48*(3), 69–76.

Honig, A. S. (1994a). Parent involvement in the early years. *Montessori Life, 6*(3), 39–42.

Honig, A. S. (1994b). Socioemotional development. In H. Nuba, M. Searson, & D. Sheiman (Eds.), *Resources for early childhood: A handbook* (pp. 51–76). New York: Garland Publishing.

Honig, A. S., & Lally, J. R. (1981). *Infant caregiving : A design for training.* Syracuse, NY: Syracuse University Press.

Honig, A. S., & Wittmer, D. S. (1992). *Prosocial development in children: Caring, sharing, and cooperation: A bibliographic resource guide.* New York: Garland Press.

Kaplan, L. (1978). *Oneness and separateness.* New York: Simon & Schuster.

Kobak, D. (1979). Teaching children to care. *Children Today, 8,* 6–7, 34–35.

Kuebli, J. (1994). Research in review: Young children's understanding of everyday emotions. *Young Children, 49*(3), 36–47.

Lewis, M., & Saarni, C. (Eds.). (1985). *The socialization of emotions.* New York: Plenum.

Lickona, T. (1983). *Raising good children: Helping your child through the stages of moral development.* New York: Bantam.

Patterson, G. R. (1984). Aggression, altruism and self-regulation. In M. H. Bornstein, & M. E. Lamb (Ed.), *Developmental psychology: An advanced textbook.* Hillsdale, NJ: Erlbaum.

Pines, M. (1979). Good samaritans at age two? *Psychology Today, 13,* 66–77.

Shure, M. B. (1992). *I can problem solve (Vol. 1 for preschool).* Champaign, IL: Research Press.

Smilansky, S., & Shefatya , L. (1990). *Facilitating play: A medium for promoting cognitive, socio-emotional and academic development in young children.* Gaithersburg, MD: Psychosocial and Educational Publications.

Smith, C. A. (1993). *The peaceful classroom: 162 easy activities to teach preschoolers compassion and cooperation.* Mt. Rainier, MD: Gryphon House.

Sroufe, L. A. (1979). Socioemotional development. In J. D. Osofsky (Ed.), *Handbook of infant development* (pp. 462–516). New York: Wiley.

Teyber, E. (1992). *Helping children cope with divorce.* New York: Lexington Books.

Thomas, A., & Chess, S. (1977). *Temperament and development.* New York, NY: Brunner/ Mazel.

Welsh, R. S. (1976, Spring). Violence, permissiveness and the overpunished child. *Journal of Pediatric Psychology,* 68–71.

Wittmer, D. S., & Honig, A. S. (1990). Teacher re-creation of negative interactions with toddlers. In A. S. Honig (Ed.), *Optimizing early child care and education* (pp. 77–88). London: Gordon & Breach.

CHAPTER 4

Learning Styles in Preschool Children

KAREN H. NELSON

Learning or cognitive styles received considerable attention during the 1960s and 1970s, but received little attention from practitioners during much of the 1980s. However, a number of factors has influenced the resurgence of interest in style. First, the rise of cognitive science has emphasized the relationship between technology and the learner, framing new questions about the interaction between the environment and the learner. Second, the concepts of cognitive style prevalent in the 1960s and 1970s have been supplemented by interest in information-processing mode, hemispheric specialization, temperament, and creativity. Third, the concept of developmental continuity has led to a reexamination of the ways in which behavior during the preschool years may be related to subsequent learning success. And fourth, research on women has contrasted a connected, relational mode with a more

KAREN H. NELSON is professor of Psychology and former dean of Social Science at Austin College, Sherman, Texas. Her doctoral dissertation from Harvard Graduate School of Education is titled *Relational Understanding in Young Children.* As Research Director of the Center for Psychological Development in Sherman, she works with a group of therapists providing consultation in developmental phenomena, in-service training in self-esteem building, uses of psychological type in educational arenas, and family systems analysis.

separate, analytical mode, a contrast that may require a re-thinking of some of the assumptions in the traditional style literature. My purposes in this chapter are to examine the models of learning style in the context of these changes since the early style research began, to speak to cultural differences and curriculum issues in responding to style, and to examine approaches to training librarians, parents, and teachers to be more style-sensitive.

Learning Styles and School Readiness

Why ought we to include learning style as a factor in deter-mining school readiness? Cullen (1991) reports a study of pre-primary children in Western Australia. Table 1 summarizes the characteristics that she examined.

TABLE 1

Metacognitive Dimensions of Strategic
Behavior in Young Children

Task persistence—extends activity, returns to activity, task inter-ruptions, flitting, socially oriented

Use of resources—experiments with resources, uses additional re-sources to solve problem

Use of peers as a resource—asks for help, cooperation

Use of adults as a resource—asks for help, responds positively to adult prompts

Self as a resource for others—helps others, gives verbal or noverbal, positive response to request for assistance

Self-regulation—inner-directed language that indicates direction of the self

Other-regulation—social language that indicates direction of others

(Cullen, 1991, p. 47)

The children labeled as "high readiness" revealed a more strategic approach to learning in preschool and continued to do so in their first year of school. High-readiness children attended more to the teacher and complied better with her instructions; they were more intentional and effective in their use of outdoor space, and they exhibited more social direction in outdoor play with peers. Not surprisingly, teachers rated these high-readiness children as having superior work habits, physical skills, and school adjustment. Although Cullen found substantial continuity between preschool and primary school behavior, she noted that sometimes discontinuity in use of learning strategies occurred; that is, children whose strategies in pre-primary classes were successful used strategies that were not successful in school and vice versa. When such discontinuity occurred, it may have been influenced by the setting in which the activity occurs, the social context, the teacher's management style, or the nature of the task. Cullen concludes:

> The learning strategies which have been identified in this study may be regarded as precursors of adaptive metacognitive abilities which enable children to monitor and regulate their own learning. . . . When children proceed to more abstract tasks at school it is important that teachers actively assist them to develop a parallel set of skills for coping with the new demands of school learning (1991, p. 52).

Cullen's work suggests, then, that there are basic differences in school readiness that derive from the strategies preschool children bring to their learning environment. Such individual differences in strategies can be examined as learning styles or cognitive styles that young children acquire as they interact with the world around them.

Galotti (1994, p. 414) begins her discussion of cognitive style by defining it in terms of individual differences:

> One way that individuals may differ from one another cognitively . . . is in terms of their *cognitive style,* their habitual or preferred means of approaching tasks (Globerson & Zelniker, 1989; Tyler, 1974). The term *cognitive style* is meant to imply certain personality and motivational factors

that influence the way in which a person approaches a cognitive task (Kogan 1983).

Traditionally, cognitive style was also seen as value free; either end of the continuum was seen as valid and valuable. It was intended to replace or supplement ideas that a child was smart or not smart, skilled or unskilled.

Problems with Learning Style Definitions

Shortly it will become clear that this view was never actually manifest in much of the research and implementation of cognitive style, but it was central to the idea of learning styles. Like many other contemporary authors, Galotti discusses field dependence-independence and reflection-impulsivity as cognitive styles. Since these were the most prominent styles in the early literature, I am going to use them both to clarify how style is defined and to identify the problems with these traditional approaches in working with preschool children. Field dependence versus independence is regarded as the first cognitive style dimension (Witkin, Dyk, Faterson, Goodenough, & Karp, 1962), Witkin's original research having begun in the 1940s. Galotti's summary of differences between field dependents and independents reflects the mix of perceptual and cognitive functioning with interpersonal skills that was presumed to describe both children and adults. Field dependents are defined as:

- less able perceptually to divorce the embedded picture from its context. . . .

- [relying on] external [field-dependent] referents in processing information from the self and the surrounding field. . . .

- more likely to rely on others, especially in ambiguous social situations.

(Galotti, 1994, pp. 414–415)

However, authors often attribute a much broader range of characteristics to field dependents and independents. Sara-

cho & Spodek (1984), for example, add to the characteristics
of field dependents listed above: "global, undifferentiated;"
"impulsive;" "sociable;" and "conforming to the effects of the
prevailing field" (p. 2). In contrast, field independents are
"analytic, differentiated;" "socially detached, removed, cold,
distant, oriented toward active striving and self-aware" (p. 2).
These characteristics are discussed in the context of research
on children's cognitive styles and raise a number of questions
about how style is measured to yield valid inferences of these
kinds. Since field dependence seems to reflect a lack of cognitive skills and a preoccupation with social relationships, are
all young children field dependent? Do differences in how
children perceive information, such as a story being read, tell
us which children are sociable and conforming and which are
cold and detached? The fact that this style includes a reference to impulsivity also raises the question of whether field
dependence is the same thing as impulsivity as measured by
what was called conceptual or cognitive tempo.

Cognitive Tempo

Cognitive tempo differentiates reflection from impulsivity,
usually by examining children's errors and latency to respond.
Impulsive children make many errors and have a very short
latency of response; reflective children make few errors while
responding slowly. While this dimension is defined in terms of
errors and latency of response, Bomba, Broberg, & Moran
(1987) find errors to be related to activity, adaptability, and
distractibility. Concern about attention deficit disorders has
stimulated substantial research on cognitive tempo. Not surprisingly, Galotti cites developmental differences in both
psychological differentiation and cognitive tempo: younger
children are more impulsive and field dependent than older
children. Globerson & Zelniker (1989) elaborate further on
the notion that there are advantages of field independence
and reflection in relation to Piagetian stages and cognitive development. Yet Steele (1989) and Saracho & Spodek (1984)
raise significant questions about measurement of cognitive
tempo and field dependence-independence, respectively. Note
however, that to say that schools favor field independence and

reflection may be a consequence of the twenty-year-old, out-dated notions of school readiness. Field independents and reflectives do very well at decontextualized tasks; they do better than their counterparts when asked to "sit down, shut up, and do what you're told." What is less clear is how well their strategies work in more contextualized situations that emphasize cooperative learning, and active engagement with materials and people.

Information-Processing Models of Learning Style

Additional models of learning style differentiate modes of in-formation processing. This approach usually contrasts prefer-ences for visual, auditory, and kinesthetic information. O'Neil (1990) argues that, when teaching strategy is matched to the student's personal learning style, both scholastic achievement and self-confidence are increased. Dunn's Learning Style In-ventory is the most commonly used instrument employing an information processing mode. However, Springer & Deutsch (1993), like O'Neil (1990), raise the possibility that it is the at-tention from interested adults that children respond to more than the matching of teaching strategy to preferred learning mode. O'Neil further questions the extent to which children know which modality they prefer. I am also convinced that each modality is much more complicated than earlier research suggested and that each modality interacts with experience. The child who has no experience with kinesthetic learning may not know that is his strength. The child who loves car-toons may report that she learns more from watching than from listening. When we say a child prefers visual processing, does that mean images of concrete objects, like the picture on a page that may cue a young child's memory for the words that are on that page, or can it mean images of words or of actions? Is there a difference among children who have vari-ous auditory preferences for repetition, alliteration, or rhym-ing? May one child's kinesthetic preference favor acting out the story as it's read, while another favors being permitted to walk around the room or doodle during story time? We do not yet have clear answers to these questions.

The modality approach has been sustained, in part, by interest in hemispheric specialization. In their remarks about hemispheric specialization and learning style, Springer & Deutsch (1993) also talk about *dichotomania,* the tendency in the popular literature to see everything as fitting neatly into either the right hemisphere or the left. The usual dichotomies include the following:

Left hemisphere	*Right hemisphere*
Verbal	Nonverbal, visuospatial
Sequential, temporal, digital	Simultaneous, spatial, analogical
Logical, analytical	Gestalt, synthetic
Rational	Intuitive
Western thought	Eastern thought

(Springer and Deutsch, 1993, p. 272)

Springer & Deutsch note that the descriptions near the top seem to have experimental evidence to support them. Note also that the earlier distinction between field-dependent and field-independent children seemed to be guilty of dichotomania, as if each style subsumed a huge set of characteristics that were the exact opposite of children with the alternative style. Springer & Deutsch cite research on rural Hopi Indians, urban blacks, rural and urban whites, then suggest that the differential performance of Hopis and blacks that was attributed to differences in cognitive style could equally easily be attributed to differences in verbal IQ. Their concern is that, if the left brain-right brain labels are a subtle way to describe verbal intelligence score, a style approach to curriculum may be of little value.

My broader concern is that, if field independence and reflection are code words for IQ or being smart, why should we bother learning new jargon? Ultimately, I believe that various styles can produce school success, but only if we do not focus on only one pole of each dimension. Springer & Deutsch note that a small number of studies has used dichotic listening and EEG measures of asymmetry, but that the question of hemisphericity relative to culture is not yet answered. With sophisticated technology available for precise measurement of brain activity and behavior, it is not surprising that Springer & Deutsch raise further concerns about the use of questionnaires to assess hemisphericity as a dimension of cognitive style, an issue that also applies to the temperament approach to style to which I will now turn.

Temperament Approaches
to Analyzing Style

O'Neil (1990) also contrasts "sensing feelers" and "abstract sequentials," a distinction reminiscent both of research on hemispheric specialization and of research on the Myers Briggs Type Indicator (MBTI) (Keirsey & Bates, 1984; Kroeger & Thuesen, 1988; Lawrence, 1993; Tieger & Barron-Tieger, 1992). Like many of the measures of style (see O'Neil, 1990) and hemisphericity (see Springer & Deutsch, 1993), the Myers Briggs type is assessed by paper-and-pencil test. Recently the Murphy-Meisgeier Type Indicator for Children has been developed, claiming to assess type in children as young as eight years, the age at which Steele (1989) claims field dependence-independence and reflection-impulsivity become stable (Meisgeier & Murphy, 1987). However, in a recent study of 513 students eight to eleven years old, two associates and I concluded that the MMTIC fails to capture stable type in many children (Nelson, LaBrie, & Carter, 1994). There was strong evidence to suggest that the climate in the classroom dictated more about how children answered the questions than their own learning preferences did.

A number of studies of style ask either the parent or the teacher to complete a simple questionnaire appraising the child's style (Birrell, Phillips, & Stott, 1985; Clark, Griffing, & Johnson, 1989). Gregorc (in O'Neil, 1990) raises strong concerns about using instruments rather than behavior to assess style. I worry not only that questionnaires may not capture the child's actual learning style, but also that young children's strategies are not yet stable enough to justify assessing style. Instead, I would recommend programs that are aimed at illustrating to parents, teachers, and children that there are many equally valid ways of learning. This "cafeteria" approach allows the child to "play" with different strategies and see them as parts of a repertoire, rather than as rigid scripts that she is "supposed" to follow.

Another approach to temperament (Lundsteen, 1985) uses M. Rosenberg's definitions of four different learning styles: rigid-inhibited, undisciplined, acceptance-anxious, and creative to study young children's performance on a prereading task involving a wordless picture book. Lundsteen concludes that style is present in young children and may persist or change over time, but has an impact on comprehension. Costello & Peyton (1973), Martin (1987), Mills & Rubin (1992), O'Neil (1990) and Lee (1986) also report research that includes measures of temperament. In addition, as I have shown, some of the research on field dependence-independence, reflection-impulsivity, creativity, and hemisphericity includes assumptions about style-temperament interactions.

Those studies allow me to make several observations about the use of a temperament approach to learning style. First, many of the temperament labels don't sound value free. Given a choice, I would rather not be called rigid-inhibited or undisciplined. Many of the labels and descriptions also seem to imply deficiency; field-dependent children are not yet independent; impulsive children have not yet learned to be reflective, and so on. If you use a temperament approach, be careful what words you choose. There is substantial evidence that when teachers perceive children as slow, they think they are stupid, and when parents and teachers label children as difficult, the children have more adjustment problems. Furthermore, if you use a temperament approach, you need to use a family systems model. No child develops a temperament or style in a vacuum. For example, Asher (1987) reviews work on shyness by Jerome Kagan, Stephen Suomi, and Philip Zimbardo. Taken together, their research suggests that while genetic predisposition may favor shyness, parents and siblings may play major roles in determining how the shyness is expressed and the extent to which it serves ultimately as an asset or a liability.

Creativity and Learning Style

Creativity has also been examined in relation to style. Broberg & Moran (1988) examined the relationship between conceptual tempo and creativity. They found no differences between reflective and impulsive preschoolers in ideational fluency, a measure of creative idea production or originality. First, they categorized preschoolers as fast-accurate, fast-inaccurate, slow-accurate, and slow-inaccurate; then they compared their performances on the creativity task. The fast-accurate and slow-inaccurate children had higher scores for originality than the remaining children. Broberg and Moran suggest that the slow-accurate children (reflectives) may be so anxious and preoccupied about getting the right answer, and the fast-inaccurates (impulsives) may lack attention to detail, motivation and persistence; as a result, these children have lower originality scores. Note that, while the early research led quickly to the inference that being reflective is good and being impulsive is bad, this research challenges that assumption. Neither the reflectives nor the impulsives were especially creative.

In a different approach to creativity, Clark, Griffing, & Johnson (1989) look at the idea of a "divergent cognitive style." They discuss the theoretical importance of play during the preschool years and propose "that the freedom and fluidity of symbolic play in the activity domain should be related to measures of creativity" (p. 77). Their review and critique of the literature are excellent and their own findings complex. In a longitudinal study of children four-and-a-half to seven-and-a-half years old, they found that for the sample as a whole and for boys, but not for girls, symbolic play in preschool related to ideational fluency in preschool and to flexibility, originality, and intelligence three years later. They propose a sleeper effect as a possible explanation, an idea which raises questions about what we expect in terms of continuity.

Sroufe (1978) notes that developmental psychologists have tended to look at continuity as the manifestation of the same behavior at two different points in time. In reviewing attachment of babies to their caregivers, he proposes that we ought instead to look for relative adaptability of a behavior. Securely attached children, for example, often cry in the presence of strangers at eight to ten months, are attracted by the novel and the complex at two years, and adjust readily to the peer group and later to school. If we use crying as the behavior we examine, we hope that we will find little continuity. Similarly, the preschooler who engages in a lot of make-believe play may not continue to play in this fashion in elementary school and may instead manifest originality in quite different ways in second grade. Such contemporary approaches to intelligence as Gardner's *Frames of Mind: The Theory of Multiple Intelligence* (1993) and Sternberg's *Beyond IQ: A Triarchic Theory of Human Intelligence* (1985) suggest a wide array of skills that are developing in young children. Gardner describes "waves," "streams," and "channels" that create a complex ebb and flow of interests, abilities, and predispositions. The five-year-old learning to read may seem to favor certain verbal, visual, and auditory skills that are very different from the tactile-kinesthetic, verbal, and visual-spatial skills necessary to acquire the concept of number six months to a year later. Gardner (1991) also highlights the complex interaction of developmental transition and learning style that must be taken into account especially in an era with as many transitions as the one that spans preschool to early elementary school.

Working with Preschoolers' Learning Styles

In the end, we can ask several questions about continuity of learning style: Do preschoolers have learning styles? Yes, I am certain that they do. Are those styles stable? Maybe or, at least in some children, they may well be. Can we assess them? Probably not reliably and quickly; a reliable and valid assessment will take time and multiple appraisals of the child in different contexts. Does that mean that those working with young children can afford to be ignorant of style? No, I don't think so.

Research on the Gender Factor

One reason it is important that we continue to grapple with the implications of learning styles for children is that the contemporary world requires professionals to be much more sensitive to issues of gender and culture. The traditional research on cognitive style frequently found gender differences, girls being more field dependent, boys more field independent; girls more reflective, boys more impulsive. The hemispheric-ity research has always been a problem for people wanting to fit specialization with gender since girls were seen as having better verbal skills (a left hemisphere task) but better non-verbal and intuitive skills (right hemisphere), while boys had better visuospatial skills (right hemisphere) but more analytical and rational skills (left hemisphere) (Halpern, 1992). O'Neil's (1990) sensing feelers and abstract sequentials sound more like girls and boys, respectively. With the flurry of gender research inspired by Gilligan (1982) and Belenky, Clinchy, Goldberger & Tarule (1986), the "dichotomania" that began with cognitive style and hemispheric specialization continued in the realm of gender.

Not surprisingly, cognitive style and gender have already been examined by some researchers. Steele (1989) compared gifted preschoolers with preschoolers not selected as gifted. She found that gifted children were more often field independent, especially the gifted girls, and gifted children were more likely to be reflective, especially the gifted boys. This research supports the earlier assertion that, developmentally, impulsive, and field dependent styles are more immature. What is intriguing is that the data also suggest that gifted children violate the expectations of their gender; that is, gifted boys and boys who are not selected as gifted are about equally field independent, but gifted girls are significantly more field independent than other girls. Conversely, gifted girls and girls not selected as gifted are about equally reflective, but gifted boys are substantially more reflective than the other boys. The theory and research on gender must be taken into account if we reexamine cognitive style.

Galotti (1994) provides an outstanding review of the methodological issues involved in studying gender differences and the caution with which we must draw inferences from gender research. Additionally, the world of education has moved far more in the direction of balance between the "separate" and "connected" modes of knowing (Belenky et al., 1986) and between reasoning that focuses on "justice and fairness" as opposed to that which is more "relational and responsive" (Gilligan, 1982; Halpern, 1992). Paley, Honig, Reifel, and Teale all speak to aspects of this approach: Paley by showing the connectional benefits of storytelling that fit with field-dependent and right-brain styles; Honig in saying that we need kids who are agentic and competent, kind and compassionate; Reifel in describing both the justice approach Piaget and Kohlberg took to moral reasoning, and in addressing the gender shifts in the last several decades that have altered what and how girls and boys may play acceptably; and Teale in referring to the power of narrative in children's lives.

Questioning the Research

Let me summarize several themes that pervade the research on learning styles. First, there is substantial concern about measurement and effective means of identifying style, especially in young children. Second, there is also concern about avoiding dichotomania while not ignoring the potential overlap of styles—are field independents always left-hemisphere dominant and reflective? Can you be reflective and right-hemisphere dominant? Can you be right-hemisphere dominant and not at all creative? Few studies have attempted to tease out the unique components of different style dimensions. Sperry (1972) and Globerson & Zelniker (1989) assert that style is not unitary, but no research to date has convincingly demonstrated that measurement error could not account for the differences in different styles. Third, the research literature has not successfully responded to the concern that learning styles are more palatable names for haves and have-nots. Field independents have skills that dependents lack; reflectives have skills that impulsives lack; and so on. The theory says that it is equally valid to be field dependent, impulsive, right brain, relational, or connectional. Is that true in the classroom? Not often. Is it true in the adult work place? Absolutely. Field-dependent employees are sensitive to the social cues around them; impulsive employees make quick decisions; right-brain employees have an intuitive grasp of the "big picture;" and relational or connectional employees regard the work environment as a vibrant, dynamic system in which people matter. Nevertheless, Birrell, Phillips, & Stott (1985) argue that learning style assessed by teachers at the end of the first year of school is highly predictive of educational achievement two years later. They also report:

Correlations between learning style and educational achievement are comparable with those between IQ and attainment, despite the advantages of contemporaneity and ap-
proximately normal distribution in all reports of the latter.
The present finding, for the early school years, suggests that
learning style correlates more highly with attainment than
does IQ, when attainment is measured later. (p. 215)

Steele (1989) also asserts that "learning style may ultimately be more important as a determinant of school success
than intelligence quotient (IQ)" (p. 158). Gardner (1991)
concurs that features of temperament and learning style that
may well influence how a child approaches learning are likely
to have been consolidated by the end of the preschool years.
What we do not yet know is whether the attainment Steele
refers to being measured is based purely on the kind of testing
that favors the field-independent, reflective style. However,
O'Neil (1990) indicates that:

many advocates say so-called "at-risk" students—those
whose personal behaviors, past educational records, or family problems increase the chance of failure—have the most
to gain from style-based learning. (p. 5)

What we have, then, is substantial concern about the
validity of measures of learning style in the context of substantial belief in the promise of learning styles. The subtle
implication of this work is that some styles accompany success. Not surprisingly, the styles that correlate with traditional school success are those that most often characterize
white, middle-class males. That observation has led very naturally to the study of cultural diversity.

Cultural Diversity and
Learning Style Research

Much of the research on learning styles has addressed cultural
diversity. Testimony before the U.S. Senate describes culturally

relevant early education programs for native Hawaiian and Navajo children (Congress of the United States, 1988). Lee (1986) reports that "American public schools value the analytical learning styles. . . . Black children, on the other hand, usually are proficient in relational learning styles. . . . [R]elational learners fail in school far more often than analytical learners do." (p. 81) Haley (1982) found that socioeconomically advantaged black preschoolers were more verbally creative and their disadvantaged black peers were more kinetically creative. Both sociodrama and verbal problem-solving exercises enhanced kinetic expressiveness but did not enhance verbal creativity. Hsia (1981) summarizes limited evidence that Asian American children are more field independent than their Caucasian peers. In another study of Asian children, Saville-Troike (1987) studied young Chinese, Japanese, and Korean children, contrasting inner-directed and outer-directed learner types. She finds that the inner-directed learners often go through a "silent" period in second language acquisition in which they seem to be using only single words in English but are, in fact, intensely studying English language use in speakers. Laosa (1980) finds the field-dependent cognitive style more common in Chicano children.

Diversity has also been addressed in a number of studies of other populations. Friedman (1983) argues that for handicapped children to benefit maximally from school, there must be an interaction between the child's learning style and effective teaching methods. Rodríguez (1984) makes a similar plea regarding teaching literacy to second language learners. O'Neil (1990) wisely notes, however, widespread concern that research on diversity only promotes cultural stereotyping. It is important not to use a learning style approach as a vehicle for prejudging children. Ultimately, one of the advantages of a learning style approach, if it is well done, is that the styles are described without emphasis on culture, class, or gender.

The confounding of socioeconomic status and culture is not easily overcome. Some of the learning style work has been very patronizing and not especially useful. Notice the child-blaming and pejorative tone in this next quotation. Costello & Peyton (1973) examined learning styles in disadvantaged children and found:

children who were *not* developing their full range of competencies were often ignoring, avoiding, or restricting their
approach to experiences in ways which temperamental
characteristics did not seem to adequately explain. In
searching for a way to understand the nature and intensity
of their involvements, we were aware that *selection and
attention* to relevant stimuli in the environment were very
basic considerations. We observe, in varying degrees, *children who look but see little, who listen but do not hear,
who touch but do not feel.* (p. 3)

More recent research suggests some of the reasons why
they may have found this. Gunarsa (1984) reports a study
in Jakarta that finds that children of higher socioeconomic
status have "better facilities, a more stimulating environment,
and more varied life experiences." (p. 1) Not surprisingly,
these children begin to speak earlier than their lower socioeconomic status peers. Although Costello & Peyton are pointing to important issues, they are doing so in a negative way,
whereas Gunarsa is noting accurately the very real differences
in early environment and experience that may explain why
some differences emerge related to socioeconomic status.

Style-Sensitive Education

The "culturally compatible education" set as the goal of the
reports to the Congress of the United States (1988) may also
mean style-sensitive education. Several studies illustrate that
when teachers are ignorant of style differences in children,
they may do the children a real disservice. Guilmet (1979)
compared Navajo and Caucasian preschool children. The
Navajo children were described as more teacher-oriented,
nonverbal help-seekers; Caucasians were more peer-oriented,
verbal help-seekers. Nevertheless, Guilmet found that teachers and teacher aides spoke to Caucasian children nearly
twice as often as to Navajo children, while ignoring Navajo
children more often than Caucasians. He further explains that
the interactional style of the Navajo mothers leads naturally
to the children's behaviors, but that the teachers were seemingly ignorant of the Navajo style. They appeared to be

annoyed by the style the mothers had intentionally socialized in their children. This finding might lead one to suspect that a match of teacher style to pupil style is always best for the child.

However, research by Laosa (1980) substantially complicates this picture. He looked at cognitive style development in five-year-old Chicano children using the field dependent-independent model of style. He finds that whereas field-independent mothers used inquiry and praise more often, field-dependent mothers used modeling more often. Further, mothers who used more positive physical control were more field independent, while those who used negative physical control were relatively field dependent. He cites earlier research by Moore (1977, in Guilmet, 1979) that found that field-independent classroom teachers used a self-discipline approach more often than did field-dependent teachers. His research was aimed at discovering whether mothers were responding to the styles of their children or imposing their own styles on the children. While there was limited support for the notion that mothers were matching their strategies to the children's styles, more compelling evidence suggested that the mothers were using strategies consistent with their own, not their children's styles. Note that while Chicano children are more often field dependent, their mothers can be either field dependent or field independent in style. Note also that the field-dependent style that is viewed as more sociable and responsive in these Chicano mothers was accompanied by the more controlling and punitive approach to discipline.

Saracho & Spodek (1984) provide further evidence of this difference in teaching and discipline style. Saracho in 1980 had studied second- and fifth-grade teachers, finding that it was field-dependent teachers who gave more negative assessments of both field-independent and field-dependent children. We might have expected either that teachers would favor children who matched their own styles or might be more tolerant of children who mismatched them in style. Saracho found that field-independent teachers were less negative than their field-dependent colleagues about field-independent children, but they were more positive about field-dependent students than the field-dependent teachers were. Saracho & Spodek (1984) find complex interactions of teacher style with both the gender and style of the child. They conclude that teachers need to be far better trained in assessing children's styles so that they can appropriately respond to them. When parents and teachers are encouraged to consider learning style as one explanation for children's differences, it is also possible that they will naturally become more self-aware about their own styles and more tolerant of styles that are different from their own.

Style and New Learning Media

Since our purpose is to examine the implications of learning style for school readiness, it seems imperative to take into account notions about cognitive development in young children that were not widely addressed when the first research on cognitive and learning styles was done. A review of just a few of the studies will raise important questions about learning style for contemporary preschoolers. Welch (1982) was one of the first sources to speak to the effect of learning from television. Since "Sesame Street" is now twenty-five years old, we face dealing with preschoolers whose parents grew up watching "educational television." It is imperative that we understand whether children benefit from the education that television and other visual media are allegedly providing. Welch notes that young children may watch visual messages but not spontaneously attach verbal labels to what they watch and may not benefit from visual material that lacks a conceptual frame provided by language. Interestingly, she points out that a child has to be watching the television to "get" the visual message but can be doing something else and still hear an auditory message. Her study revealed, however, that visual information has priority for preschoolers. Those exposed to visual information and audiovisual information remembered substantially more than those exposed to auditory information.

Note, however, that Welch does not consider the possibility of style differences in children. Are there "auditory" learners who fail to benefit from visual material that lacks an auditory frame and vice versa? Cuffaro (1984) adds:

> Though self-evident, it is worth noting that the microcom-
> puter also introduces a particular learning style into the
> school setting of young children—the familiar posture of
> television viewing. (pp. 561–562)

She raises two important issues regarding the use of microcomputers with preschoolers, both of which highlight the
extent to which technological advances do not occur in a
vacuum. First, the microcomputer as an adjunct to foster
learning must reflect and be consistent with the teacher's
organizing structure and the teacher must examine *how* it
reflects his or her style. Second, Cuffaro asks that educators
think carefully about how children who are not yet concrete
operational in Piagetian terms can work with computers. We
cannot simply take strategies that are appropriate for older
children and expect younger children to adopt them when
they work with a microcomputer.

Davis & Pepper (1992) illustrate a more recent approach
to the study of strategies in early work with mathematics.
They argue that children's early responses are "unlearned"
and that there is a diversity of solution strategies that children
unselfconsciously bring to simple dealing or sharing tasks and
redistributing. For example, a new child joins a trio who have
divided a dozen cookies among them; how can they give the
fourth child his or her fair share? Although Davis & Pepper
contrast "good and poor counters," a learning style approach
might be equally useful in categorizing children's strategies
without linking strategy to success or failure. In addition to
television, microcomputers, and mathematics, language instruction may also be adapted readily to learning style.

Pramling (1992) sees real value in having children come
to understand their own learning process. She begins her
analysis as follows:

> There are two dominant perspectives within the field of
> early childhood education. The first one focuses on chil-
> dren's development as an internally driven process. . . . The
> other perspective is borrowed from the ordinary school sys-
> tem and views children's learning as a transference of skills
> and knowledge from outside the child. (p. 2)

She argues that an experiential approach to children's apprehension of meaning will respond both to their need for learning and for development, which she sees as inseparable. A rich and vital reading program is a perfect example of such experiential approaches.

Linking Preschool Styles
with School Performance

If learning style is to be helpful in assessing and developing school readiness, we must also know the relationship between early style and later school performance. Here the research is complex, forcing an examination of the role of developmental status in style, the need for broader notions of developmental continuity, and the possibility that early style plays a major role in later metacognitive strategies. As early as 1974, Sklerov contrasted sixteen children who had participated in Project Head Start with sixteen who had not. The Head Start children showed much more reflective behavior—significantly longer times and significantly lower error scores. If exposure to pre-school education helps children become more reflective, and older children are both more reflective, and more field independent, we quickly run into the challenge of deciding when education serves to facilitate development and when it merely imposes a style that is valued more highly by the school. Steele (1989) tackles the even more complicated question of what to do with gifted preschoolers. She was cited earlier as asserting that learning style may be even more important than intelligence in determining school success. Having documented the relative stability of cognitive style from age eight to adulthood, she asks:

> If the gifted child of four to six has a MA or developmental age of six to eight years, has the cognitive style of the gifted young child already begun to stabilize? . . . Endowed with one or more of such unique abilities, will gifted preschoolers who are more cognitively able be more reflective and field independent at an earlier age than those persons not selected as gifted-and-talented? (p.159)

Her answer is in the affirmative:

> The cognitive style of the gifted young child is clearly dis-
> cernable from chronological peers. Preschool gifted chil-
> dren are more likely to be field independent—especially
> girls, and more likely than their CA peers to be reflective—
> especially boys. (p.170)

Does this mean that if we adopt a learning style approach
to school readiness, we will decide that we value field independence and reflectivity even if that means suppressing
the child's natural style? Lee (1986), examining "The match:
Learning styles of black children and microcomputer programming," argues: "Successful people use not only their
preferred learning style, but they integrate and harmonize different styles within their cognitive structures so that they can
function in different settings for various reasons and can complete many diverse kinds of tasks." (p. 81) The "cafeteria"
approach I mentioned earlier is one means of following Lee's
advice. If we regard field dependence and field independence
or auditory and visual learning as alternative strategies, each
of which is highly valuable in some situations, we naturally
expose children to strategies that they can add to their repertoire. One's natural strategy may still emerge first, and when
one is under stress or in a novel situation, but alternative
strategies can be brought to bear when they are adaptive.

Globerson & Zelniker (1989) ask whether style is a matter
of information-processing preference in which each preference can be enabling, or whether it is merely another way to
describe ability. They note that while the early research on
style claimed no value judgment about which style is better,
subsequent research found specific styles were correlated
with "measures of general intelligence, problem-solving abilities, cognitive development, and school achievement in certain domains." (p.7) They report research that children can
be given "style-appropriate" instruction and perform equally
well in some tasks. One good example of diverse successful
styles relates to reading. Kurt Fischer, speaking at the American Psychological Association convention in San Francisco in
1991, reported data finding that equally competent third-

grade readers sometimes started reading at four, sometimes at eight, and sometimes in between. Increasingly, developmental psychology is examining alternative trajectories that may yield quite different paths to the same end.

In addition, however, style-appropriate methods will need to balance the desire to provide rich stimulation of different trajectories without creating information-processing overload. In preschool there are many pairs of activities children cannot do at one time. One example is based on Vygotsky. Preschoolers and early elementary school children were given a task which required learning that if one light bulb flashed, the child should press a button; if the other light flashed, the child should not press the button. What Zivin found was that for most preschoolers, language had not yet become a tool in service of problem solving. Some preschoolers were taught the rule, "Red means stop, green means go. If the red light comes on, don't push the button, but if the green light comes on push it." Other preschoolers were not taught the rule. Similarly, some early elementary children were taught the rule and others were not. Zivin found that preschoolers mastered the task faster when they were not taught the rule, whereas elementary children learned it faster when they repeated it as a self-instruction. For the younger children, the "rule" created an overload; developmentally, more is not always better.

Style-Sensitivity and Flexibility

If we are going to use a learning-style approach to preschool readiness, can style-sensitivity be taught? Learning style can become a natural vehicle for developing the metacognitive abilities that will be necessary in school. To do that we need only look at alternative facets of style as different strategies, equally valid options that may be more or less adaptive in different settings. If a child attends an elementary school with teachers who use the traditional average wait-time of one second, the child is at a disadvantage for being reflective. When children play soccer, it is the impulsive and the occasional fast-accurate children who do well. The slower children, both accurate and inaccurate, get yelled at a lot by both parents and coaches. If we use an approach that is variously called *bicognitive development* (Saracho & Spodek, 1984), *fluid style* (Sperry, 1972) or *style flexibility,* we simply look at styles as a repertoire of strategies.

Measurement Difficulties

However, if we want to use a learning-style approach that emphasizes flexibility, there are still value biases to be overcome. Measurement was one of the earliest challenges for researchers interested in cognitive style. Much of the early research simply defined one pole of each cognitive style dimension by failure to perform successfully as those at the other pole did. Such failure approaches make it very difficult to justify style as "value-free" and make it even more difficult to differentiate style from developmental status, motivation, previous experience at home and at school, as well as other characteristics of the child. More recently, some paper-and-pencil measures have been developed, but concerns about the validity and reliability of such approaches have been raised.

Training Teachers to Recognize Styles

Do the measurement problems recommend an abandonment of the style concept? To the contrary, a number of efforts have been directed at training teachers to be able to characterize a young child's learning style. Owens (1991) summarizes a ten-week workshop providing staff training in identification of learning styles. She begins by noting that while teachers and other staff knew there were different learning styles, they had neither the skill nor the self-confidence to apply theory to actual lesson planning, instruction, and parent conferences. Martin (1987) similarly describes learning-style training for preschool teachers. Earlier this spring I decided to see how practical these approaches were. Routinely in my life span course, I have my students do child interviews at area public schools. Dr. Connie Baker, principal of Perrin Elementary School in Sherman, Texas, kindly agreed to help me with my investigation. I asked kindergarten and first-grade teachers to complete a learning-styles questionnaire, drawn from Martin's work with an added analytic-global dimension that I put in out of curiosity about hemispheric specialization research. I then had my students (juniors and seniors) do a twenty-minute exercise with the children involving a naming task, a creativity task, and storytelling by the child. The student then completed a learning-style questionnaire for the child. Note that I had trained neither the teachers nor the students in learning-style theory and research. I gave both groups simple characterizations of the poles for different styles and a seven-point scale to work with. My data are provided in Table 2.

TABLE 2

Learning Styles Data

Upper division undergraduates and the child's teacher completed a Learning Styles Questionnaire. The following compares the student's appraisal of the child with the teacher's. The data below reflect how close the two appraisals were, with = being identical, 1 reflecting one 'space' away on the 7-point scale, etc.

	Differences in appraisals							
Style variables	=	1	2	3	4	5	6	Pct = or 1 apart
Slow-fast	16	22	8	8	4	1	0	64.4%
Cautious-impulsive	17	19	8	10	3	2	0	61.0%
Regular-unpredictable	20	18	11	5	5	0	0	64.4%
Distractible-focused	11	30	10	2	4	1	1	69.5%
Intense-calm	12	24	11	1	5	4	2	61.0%
Long-short attention	21	18	8	6	4	2	0	66.1%
Reflective-reactive	13	13	17	6	8	2	0	44.1%
Analytic-global	16	20	11	4	4	3	0	62.1%

The table reports agreement between the teacher-student pairs regarding each of fifty-nine children and the percentage of cases in which my student and the teacher assigned identical ratings or ratings within one point of each other. Note that for the majority of pairs the ratings are identical or one point away in ranking. The percentages of children with the same or within-one-point rankings are provided in the right-hand column. Interestingly, only the reflective-reactive scale has a modal difference of two points. These data illustrate the promise of a learning-styles approach. Teachers can easily characterize children behaviorally in ways that are consistent with learning style. They can also develop means of teaching children strategies to enhance their ability to cope with diverse learning situations. What we need next is style-sensitive research that provides guidelines for deciding how reflective or field independent it is reasonable for us to expect a five year old to be. With those guidelines, we can then move toward behavioral assessments of style that focus on strategy training to increase children's adaptability and flexibility in diverse learning situations.

Notes for Librarians

I would like to conclude with several recommendations about learning style in library program implementation. First, don't worry about doing everything. Pick one or at most two models that make sense to you. Learn some more about them and try to figure out how to be more style-sensitive in the settings in which you work. Second, children don't need more labels. Some children have stable styles that won't change. Some are following scripts that reflect parent or sibling styles and, left to their own devices, will develop a new style. I am also reminded of the research that finds separated identical twins are often more like each other than twins who grow up together. The separation and individuation process Honig describes elsewhere in this volume is a lot easier if you work hard to be the opposite of your twin or sibling. Third, there is an ebb and flow in children's development. During transitions, quiet children often act out and active children often become quiet. Cognitively, a child may prefer language for a while, then math, then art and back to reading. Fourth, focus on strategy. What kinds of experience are intended to help impulsive children develop a longer attention span? What kinds of experience lead the more reflective or reticent child to feel safe taking risks, being a bit more spontaneous? Fifth, be careful about developing complicated agendas. It is far better to focus on a small number of objectives that make sense to the diverse constituencies with which you work. Sixth, instead of worrying about the child's style, think instead about the ways in which you can use diverse styles in your presentations in hopes that once in a while a child whose parent or teacher has a different style may discover that there is a style that affirms who they are. Finally, remember that what is most important in developing school readiness is affirming children for the skills that they have and building their confidence that they are ready for the ones they have not mastered yet.

Works Cited

Asher, J. (1987). Born to be shy? *Psychology Today, 21,* 56–59, 62–64.

Belenky, M. F., Clinchy, B. M., Goldberger, N. R., & Tarule, J. M. (1986). *Women's ways of knowing.* New York: Basic Books.

Birrell, H. V., Phillips, C. J., & Stott, D. H. (1985). Learning style and school attainment in young children: A follow-up study. *School Psychology International, 6,* 207–218.

Bomba, A. D., Broberg, G. C., & Moran, J. D. (1987). Personality correlates of conceptual tempo. Paper presented at the Annual Meeting of the Oklahoma Home Economics Association. (ERIC Document Reproduction Service No. ED 287 602)

Broberg, G. C. & Moran, J. P. (1988). Creative potential and conceptual tempo in preschool children. *Creativity Research Journal, 1,* 115–121.

Clark, P. M., Griffing, P. S., & Johnson, L. G. (1989). Symbolic play and ideational fluency as aspects of the evolving divergent cognitive style in young children. *Early Child Development and Care, 51,* 77–88.

Costello, J., & Peyton, E. (1973). The socialization of young children's learning styles. Child Study Center Report #OCD-CB-388. New Haven, CT: Yale University. (ERIC Document Reproduction Service No. ED 091 058)

Congress of the U.S., Washington DC: Senate Select Committee on Indian Affairs. (1988). *Culturally relevant early education programs.* (ERIC Document Reproduction Service No. ED 303 288)

Cuffaro, H. K. (1984). Microcomputers in education: Why is earlier better? *Teachers College Record, 85*(4), 559–568.

Cullen, J. Y. (1991). Children's learning strategies: Continuities and discontinuities. *International Journal of Early Childhood, 23*(1), 44–58.

Davis, G., & Pepper, K. (1992). Mathematical problem solving by preschool children. *Educational Studies in Mathematics, 23*(4) 397–415. Netherlands: Kluwer Academic Publishers.

Friedman, J. (1983, August). A teacher's perspective of the five P's. *The five P's: A new handicapped preschool children's assessment tool.* Paper presented at the Annual Convention of the American Psychological Association Anaheim, CA.

Galotti, K. M. (1994). *Cognitive psychology in and out of the laboratory.* Pacific Grove, CA: Brooks-Cole, pp. 414–416.

Gardner, H. (1993). *Frames of mind: The theory of multiple intelligence. Tenth-anniversary edition.* New York: Basic Books.

Gardner, H. (1991). *The unschooled mind: How children think and how schools should teach.* New York: Basic Books.

Gilligan, C. (1982). *In a different voice: Psychological theory and women's development.* Cambridge, MA: Harvard University Press.

Globerson, T, & Zelniker, T. (Eds.). (1989). *Cognitive style and cognitive development.* Norwood, NJ: Ablex.

Guilmet, G. M. (1979). Instructor reaction to verbal and nonverbal visual styles: An example of Navajo and Caucasian children. *Anthropology & Education Quarterly, 10* (4), 254–66.

Gunarsa, S. D. (1984). Cognitive development of children: Symposium IA. Research report in preparation for adulthood, 3rd Asian workshop on child and adolescent development. (ERIC Document Reproduction Service No. ED 273 356)

Haley, G. L. (1982, March). *Creative response styles: The effects of socioeconomic status and problem solving training.* Paper presented at the annual meeting of the American Educational Research Association, New York.

Halpern, D. F. (1992). *Sex differences in cognitive abilities,* 2nd edition. Hillsdale, NJ: Erlbaum.

Hsia, J. (1981). *Cognitive assessment of Asian Americans.* Professional Paper. (ERIC Document Reproduction Service No. ED 221 628)

Keirsey, D., & Bates, M. (1984). *Please understand me.* Del Mar, CA: Prometheus Nemesis.

Kroeger, O., & Thuesen, J. (1988). *Type talk.* New York: Bantam Doubleday Dell.

Laosa, L. M. (1980). Maternal teaching strategies and cognitive styles in Chicano families. *Journal of Educational Psychology, 72,* 45–54.

Lawrence, G. (1993). *People types and tiger stripes,* 3rd edition. Gainesville, FL: Center for Application of Psychological Type.

Lee, M. W. (1986). The match: Learning styles of black children and microcomputer programming. *Journal of Negro Education, 55* (1), 78–90.

Lundsteen, S.W. (1985, May). *The impact of learning/solving styles and development on young children's performance of a pre-reading task.* Paper presented at the annual meeting of the International Reading Association, New Orleans, LA.

Martin, B. B. (1987). *Developing a teaching-learning styles scheme to improve teaching behaviors of college child development interns.* Nova University practicum paper. (ERIC Document Reproduction Service No. ED 288 638)

Meisgeier, C., & Murphy, E. A. (1987). *The Murphy-Meisgeier Type Indicator for Children.* Palo Alto, CA: Consulting Psychologists Press.

Mills, R. S. L., & Rubin, K. H. (1992). A longitudinal study of maternal beliefs about children's social behaviors. *Merrill-Palmer Quarterly, 38* (4), 494–512.

Nelson, K. H., LaBrie, W. D., & Carter, M. (April 1994). *Trends in type differentiation: How age, gender and teacher type interact with students' type.* Poster presented at the meeting of the Southwestern Psychological Association, Tulsa, OK.

O'Neil, J. (1990) Making sense of style. *Educational Leadership,* 4–9.

Owens, S. J. (1991). *Establishing staff training for identifying learning styles in the preschool setting.* Practicum paper Nova University. (ERIC Document Reproduction Service No. ED 342 501)

Pramling, I. (1992, August). Oceans of meaning: Using children's ideas as content in preschool teaching. Paper presented at OMEP's World Congress Meeting, Mesa/Flagstaff, AZ.

Rodriquez, R. (Ed.). (1984). Teaching reading to language minority students. (ERIC Document Reproduction Service No. ED 338 110)

Saracho, O.N., & Spodek, B. (1984). Cognitive style and children's learning: Individual variation in cognitive processes. (ERIC Document Reproduction Service No. ED 247 034)

Saville-Troike, M. (1987). Private speech: Second language learning during the "silent" period. *Papers and Reports on Child Language Development* (Vol. 26). (ERIC Document Reproduction Service No. ED 288 373)

Sklerov, Audrey J. (1974). The effect of preschool experience on the cognitive style of reflectivity-impulsivity of disadvantaged children. *Graduate Research in Education and Related Disciplines, 7* (2), 77–91.

Sperry, L. (Ed.). (1972). *Learning Performance and Individual Differences: Essays and readings.* Glenview, IL: Scott Foresman.

Springer, S., & Deutsch, G. (1993). *Left Brain/ Right Brain,* 4th edition. New York: W. H. Freeman.

Sroufe, A. (1978). Attachment and the roots of competence. *Human Nature, 1,* 50–57.

Steele, C. (1989). Cognitive style and the gifted young child. *Early Child Development and Care, 51,* 157–174.

Sternberg, R. J. (1985). *Beyond IQ: A triarchic theory of human intelligence.* New York: Cambridge University Press.

Tieger, P., & Barron-Tieger, B. (1992). *Do what you are.* Boston, MA: Little, Brown.

Welch, A. J. (1982, May). *The impact of information channel on verbal recall among preschool aged television viewers.* Paper presented at the Annual Meeting of the Eastern Communication Association, Hartford, CT.

Witkin, H. A., Dyk, R. B., Faterson, H. F., Goodenough, D. R., & Karp, S. A. (1962). *Psychological Differentiation.* New York: Wiley.

Wright, M. J. (1978, March). *Compensatory education for pre-schoolers: A non-technical report on the U.W.O.* University of Western Ontario: London, England. (ERIC Document Reproduction Service No. ED 161 555)

CHAPTER 5

Preschool Children's
Oral and Written Language
Issues and Challenges

SARAH HUDELSON

". . . by the year 2000 all children in America will start school
ready to learn." When I first heard that statement, I became
quite nervous. I feared that some young children would be
labeled as not ready, or not willing, or not able to learn. My
study of and experience with young children's learning, particularly their language learning, convinces me that all children are active learners, that from birth children are learning
continually but learning in ways that may be different and not
recognized by many of the schools that they attend. So I
would respond to the first of the National Education Goals
with a statement that we know that all children are natural
learners, and that it is up to schools and other institutions to
understand, value, appreciate, and tap into the ways that
children learn, including how they learn in real life outside
school settings.

SARAH HUDELSON is associate professor in the Division of Curriculum
and Instruction at Arizona State University at Tempe. Her recent articles
include: "Emergent Literacy in a Whole Language Bilingual Program" in
At-Risk Students: Portraits, Policies and Programs and "The Role of Native
Language Literacy in the Education of Language Minority Children" in
Language Arts.

Our understandings need to include how children learn and use language. From this active learning perspective, then, I plan to describe what children acquire when they acquire language; how children acquire language; how children make use of language to serve their needs and desires; and differences and similarities across individuals and groups. Because the National Education Goals emphasize all children, I plan to give particular emphasis to issues of language acquisition and use across varying linguistic and ethnic and socioeconomic classes. I will also include both oral and written language development.

What Children Acquire
When They Learn to Talk

I will begin with oral language and ask: What do children acquire when they acquire oral language? From the vantage point of the mid-1990s, it is now well accepted that as children acquire the ability to speak they are essentially acquiring knowledge of the basic, underlying structures or components of the language they are learning (Lindfors, 1987). When linguists write about language structures or components of a language, they generally refer to the phonology or the component of the sounds that, in certain combinations, make up the words of any given language; the syntax or the component of the ordering of the words, how words may be strung together to create utterances; and the semantic component, the meaning system of the language, the meanings that are attached to words in any given language (Chaika, 1982). Perhaps an example or two will make these points clear.

Take this sentence: "The blugy chinzels slottled prasily on the flubbish wub" (Campbell & Lindfors, 1969, p. 106). If I were to ask you if this sentence sounded like English, you would probably agree that it does. Words have been created in accordance with the ways that sounds may be combined in English. In addition, you might note that the words make a well-formed English sentence in the sense that there is a subject (the "blugy chinzels") and a predicate (the verb phrase "slottled prasily"). Or you might use other terms to label the parts of the sentence or to refer in some way to the word order of sentence as being typical English word order. Phonologically and syntactically the sentence is English. However, if I asked you what was wrong or odd about the sentence, you probably would suggest that it's nonsense, that many of the created words do not exist in English.

Similarly if I were to ask you what is wrong with this sentence: "Colorless green ideas sleep furiously," you might also suggest that it doesn't make sense but for a different reason. The words are real English words, but they don't fit together in terms of their meanings. For English speakers, the terms "colorless" and "green" are contradictory or mutually exclusive; ideas are not animate and hence would not wake or sleep; and "sleeping" suggests a stillness while "furiously" suggests activity. As a user of English you are able to reflect on the oddities of this sentence even if you do not use the same words that I have used in your consideration of what is strange about it. You are able to do this because of your intuitive knowledge of English. It is this kind of linguistic knowledge, or what has been termed linguistic competence, that children develop as they acquire their native language. They begin to develop this knowledge long before they go to school and experience the attachment of formal labels to the language that they use (Lindfors, 1987). This kind of underlying linguistic knowledge is essential because from it children are able to generate sentences that they have never heard before.

Children's linguistic competence is related directly to the language used in the communities in which they are raised. The United States is a country of tremendous social, ethnic, and cultural diversity, and English speakers do not all speak the same dialect or variety of English. From the perspective of linguists, all dialects or varieties of English are equal linguistically, in the sense that all of them adhere to specific phonological, syntactic, and semantic rules. For example, author Lucille Clifton has used features of Black Vernacular English in some of her children's books, as in *All Us Come Cross the Water* (Clifton, 1973), in which the main character Ujamma (called Jim by his teacher) ponders his roots:

> Big Mama is my Mama's Mama's Mama. She real old and she
> don't say much, but she see things cause she born with a

veil over her face. That make it so she can see spirits and things. . . . I say, "Big Mama, will you tell me where we is all from?" I figure I got her now. She say, "Why you wanna know?" I tell her about the teacher and everybody. She say, "My Mama say her and her Mama was brought from Whydah in Dahomey in 1855."

(Clifton, 1973, n.p.)

No linguist would view children who speak a Black Vernacular English, Appalachian English, or any other variety of the language as ignorant or lazy or stupid or deficient linguistically or incorrect in their speech. Rather, they are demonstrating that they have acquired the rules for the particular variety of English that surrounds them (Labov, 1970). What is or becomes problematic for children is not the dialect itself but attitudes that teachers and others hold toward users of a "nonstandard" variety (Williams, 1980) and negative consequences for dialect users.

In addition to linguistic competence, the ability to manipulate the structures of language, children also develop what linguists call pragmatic or communicative or discourse competence, which refers to the ability to use language appropriately across social settings (Chaika, 1982; Hymes, 1974). If we think of ourselves as speakers, we can identify ways in which our speech changes according to the people with whom we are speaking, the settings in which we find ourselves, and often the topic we are discussing. The way that I speak in front of a group, for example, is quite different from the way that I would speak with my husband at home. The way that we speak in the cafeteria is different from the way that we speak at the home of the Dean of the School of Library Science. If we are talking about our families our speech may be quite different than if we are talking about library services for young children. There is significant evidence that children become aware of these differences at a young age. Lisa Delpit, a respected African American language educator, provides an example as she writes of her own experiences as a first year teacher of first-grade African American children. Her carefully rehearsed lesson presentation began, "Good morning boys and girls. Today we're going to read a story about where we live—in the city." As she spoke, a child she knew her raised her hand and commented, "Teacher how come you talkin' like a white person? You talkin' just like my momma talk when she get on the phone!" (Delpit, 1990, p. 247).

It is also true that any speech community has its own norms or rules for speaking, for what is appropriate socially and culturally. In some families or communities, for example, overlapping speech or speech characterized by almost no pauses between speakers is the norm. In other families or communities, only one person at a time speaks and the pause time between speakers is longer (Tannen, 1984). In some speech communities, lengthy verbal conclusions are required in order to terminate conversations; in other communities this is not the case. As children grow up in a particular speech community, they learn what is appropriate; they learn how to initiate, enter, sustain, and terminate conversations in ways that other members of the community deem as appropriate. They do not learn this, in most cases, by explicit instruction, but rather through observing and participating in the ongoing events and activities of their families and communities. This means that not only do children acquire the language of their communities, they are acquired by the speech community, in the sense that they are socialized into particular ways of using language that are appropriate for their communities (Johnson, 1994). Once again, this may become problematic for some children because their communities' ways of talking are not the ones accepted and valued by the schools and other institutions (Au, 1993). I will return to this issue in terms of the next questions: How and why do children learn language?

How and Why Children Learn to Talk

In the mid-1990s, it is generally accepted that language acquisition is not a process of imitation and repetition. Instead, the process is one, from infancy on, of children's construction or generation of the rules of the language for themselves. Children work to figure out how the language works. They make hypotheses or guesses about the language, about how to say what they want to say. Inevitably they create utterances that do not correspond to adult speech. Over time, however their hypotheses change and their speech, as it moves through babbling, single words, formulae, to combinatory speech, moves closer to the ways that adult members of a given community express themselves. Basically language acquisition is a process of creative construction; children are figuring out for themselves how to say what they want to say (Lindfors, 1987; Wells, 1985, 1986).

The individual child is engaged in cognitive activity that involves relating objects, events, people, and concepts in the world to specific linguistic forms. Children have to attend not only to what is happening in their worlds, but also to how those around them are expressing linguistically what is happening (Clark, 1983). But, while children's language acquisition is cognitive in nature in that it involves children in figuring the language out and in constructing the rules for their language, language acquisition is also profoundly social in nature. The view on language acquisition that is most accepted currently is the one that has been termed the *social interactionist perspective* with its focus on the social nature of language learning (Genishi & Dyson, 1984). According to this view, children acquire language as they are living in their worlds; as they are growing up in families and communities where they are figuring out how to function as family and community members; as they are accomplishing their purposes in the world. Language is one tool that children see others use and work to use themselves to participate in the world; language is one way that children have of making sense of the world and of acting in it. According to social interactionists, children, as social beings, acquire language because it is useful to them. Language is one way that children have of making and maintaining contact with others; through language children are able to have their needs meet; children use language to express both their own individuality and, simultaneously, their connections with others. Language learning and daily living are not separate spheres of activity. Children learn language as they live their daily lives in the company of other people (Lindfors, 1990).

The social interactionist perspective was grounded originally in research carried out basically with middle-class mothers and children. This research concluded that there is what Lindfors (1987) has called a mother-child jointness or partnership, characterized by mother and child working together to understand and be understood, to use talk as one way of accomplishing and mediating daily activities, and to maintain relationships and communicate with each other. There is significant evidence that in this joint work, adults (usually mothers) are especially tuned in to the child's efforts to communicate, so that they are constantly responsive to the child. Adults work hard to understand what children are trying to express. With very young children, they try to interpret the child's behaviors, such as vocalizations and gestures, as meaningful contributions to the conversation. They use repetition, expansion, extension, paraphrase, and questioning to keep conversations going. Adults often establish verbal routines or expected ways of doing things together verbally, which facilitate children's active participation in conversations. Adults tend to accept children's contributions as meaningful, no matter how unconventional their forms. And the adult's conventional responses provide linguistic data for the child to use in keeping up her end of the conversation. Thus both mother and child are focused on meaningful communication, on using language to accomplish their purposes in the world (Lindfors, 1987).

Cultural and Linguistic Diversity in Speech

For many years a major assumption of the social interactionist position on language acquisition was that the mother-child interactions just summarized occurred across social classes and ethnic or cultural groups, perhaps even across languages. But recent work has demonstrated that the kinds of adult-child social interactions depicted in much of the language acquisition literature, and assumed by many teachers to be typical interaction, since most teachers are themselves middle class, are not typical for all speech communities. In fact, there are significant differences among culturally, ethnically, and linguistically diverse communities in the patterns of interaction among community members that contribute to children's acquisition of a native language. Two of the most well researched and now well known examples are found in the work of anthropologists Shirley Brice Heath and Susan Philips.

Heath (1983) documented ways in which children, growing up in three distinct communities in the Carolina Piedmont, learned and used language within their home and neighborhood settings. The three communities were: a middle-class mainstream Anglo setting labeled Townspeople; a working-class African American community termed Trackton; and a working-class Anglo community called Roadville. While the language and learning socialization of the children in the mainstream setting were congruent with previous research settings, language learning and use for the children in the other two settings were significantly different.

In Trackton, for example, Heath found that most of community life was conducted on community members' front porches or on the plaza in the middle of the neighborhood. Even children less than 18 months old found themselves, instead of in intimate one-to-one relationships with a single adult attending to them, in the midst of groups of children and adults, where they were teased and challenged verbally by multiple interlocutors and expected to respond by performing in some way that would catch and retain an audience's interest. Preschool children, particularly young boys, were expected to be able to entertain an audience with verbal performance and to maintain that audience's interest. Many Trackton preschoolers became highly verbal, prolific storytellers.

However, as other researchers have noted, the kinds of stories produced were ones that began with one topic and led into the relating of multiple episodes related to the central theme, but with the associations to the central theme left implicit rather than being spelled out. This way of narrating has been termed *topic-associative style,* and it contrasts to *topic-centered style* narration where speakers stick to a single topic and make connections between parts of the narration very explicit (Cazden, 1988). This kind of verbal performance, so common in African American communities, has been proven by linguists to demonstrate verbal sophistication and not deprivation (Smitherman, 1977). However, it is often not appreciated in classroom settings where children are sanctioned by teachers, in activities such as show and tell and sharing time, because the children are perceived to be not narrating clearly or getting off track when narrating an event (Cazden, 1988; Heath, 1983; Michaels, 1981, 1986). Teachers who do not recognize culturally different ways of narrating often unwittingly discourage children's verbal participation because they do not acknowledge the children's ways of telling stories (Heath, 1983; Au, 1993).

Heath also discovered that in Trackton homes adults questioned children much less frequently than in the mainstream community, and that children less often were seen as conversational partners for adults. In addition, Trackton adults did not ask their preschool children questions the adults already knew the answers to, display questions, such as "What is this called?" when referring to a known item. But the children's primary grade teachers frequently asked this kind of known-answer questions and were bothered that the Trackton children were not able to answer seemingly simple questions (Heath, 1983). The children were viewed in terms of linguistic and communicative deficits.

In a different setting, Susan Philips (1983) contrasted Anglo middle-class language socialization with what she found in the Warm Springs American Indian community. She also examined and described what she termed the community's participant structures, meaning the accepted rules for how community members participated in the accomplishment of community activities. She found that, in contrast to the mainstream way of one person leading and the others following in a discussion, it was typical for community members to work together and for decisions to be reached jointly and without individuals calling attention to themselves by standing out from the group. Philips contrasted this mutuality and aversion to calling attention to oneself either verbally or behaviorally to the typical school notion of individual performance, including individual recitation. She and others have challenged the notion of the verbally deprived, silent Indian (see Cazden, John, & Hymes, 1972) as they have pointed out the significant differences between the rules for verbal participation in communities and in many schools. Children may choose not to talk in school not because they cannot talk, but because they are being asked to interact in ways that violate cultural, community norms for interaction. The more sensitive adults were to culturally accepted ways of speaking, the greater the participation; the less sensitive adults were, the less the participation (Au, 1993).

When English Is a Second Language

To this point, the examples that I have used have been of English-speaking communities. There are millions of young children in this country, however, who are being raised in households where a language other than English is spoken (Waggoner, 1992). Like all children, these learners are learning to use their native languages by living in and being socialized into particular speech communities. We have available currently only a limited amount of research done on language acquisition in languages other than English. This research suggests that, across languages, children are involved in culturally preferred ways of using language (Johnson, 1994) that are often significantly different from the "mainstream" ways into which middle-class English-speaking parents and teachers assume children will be socialized.

In terms of school readiness, one of the major issues with regard to non-English speaking learners is the role of other languages in children's learning. Often assumptions have been made, in spite of considerable research evidence speaking to the efficacy of teaching children through their native language (Ramirez, et al., 1991), that children are not ready to learn unless they are ready to learn in English. This has meant that numbers of preschool and Head Start programs have embraced the idea of an early introduction of English to preschool children, although early childhood language acquisition experts have maintained that parents should continue using the native language at home, so that children develop linguistic abilities and communicative competence in their home tongues while acquiring English (Tabors & Snow, 1994). Theoretically this situation should result in children becoming bilingual, but using their two languages in different settings; for example, using Spanish in the home and neighborhood and English at school (the diglossic situation described by Fishman, 1968).

Unfortunately the reality is that early entrance into preschools where English is used has often meant that non-English speaking children stop using their native language(s) and choose to communicate exclusively in English. Noted researcher Lily Wong Fillmore (1991) has documented this phenomenon in a study of the home language use practices of over 300 immigrant preschoolers. These children, enrolled both in English-only and bilingual preschools, were particularly vulnerable to the loss of their native language. The more time they spent in preschool settings, the more they relied on English for communication, even at home. This jeopardized non-English speaking parents' abilities to interact verbally with their children and to socialize them. While certainly non-English speaking children need to learn English in order to achieve in U.S. schools, one of the issues that Fillmore raises is whether English language acquisition has to be achieved at the expense of other languages. Her data make clear the potentially devastating consequences of children's refusals to use their native languages. How can parents nurture their children, pass on family histories and community mores, transmit cultural information, and provide their children with values to sustain them as they are confronted with dilemmas in their lives if they are unable to communicate with their children? Fillmore's work raises important questions about language loss.

From the perspective of language acquisition itself, researchers studying preschool and primary school age children's learning of a second language have discovered that, like first language acquisition, second language acquisition is both a social and a cognitive process (Fillmore, 1976). Children are involved actively in figuring out how the new language works; experimentation with the new language is necessary, and mistakes are a natural part of second language learning. Children make use of both peers and adults around them, both in terms of language input they receive and in terms of using the new language to accomplish their purposes. It is quite common for young children to go through a period when they continue to use their first language with nonspeakers of that language, often followed by a period when they do not verbalize in their new language, but rather observe closely and communicate nonverbally, using strategies such as making noises including whimpering and/or connecting with others through gestures and facial expressions (Tabors, 1987; Tabors & Snow, 1994).

Eventually, although with tremendous individual differences in both willingness to talk and in rate of acquisition of the new language (Fillmore, 1976), children begin to use English. Initially they use memorized bits of English that will allow them to participate in activities and later engage in hypothesis generating and testing as they figure out how English works. Estimates are that it will take many children at least five years before they are able to use English as native speakers do.

Given the social nature of language acquisition, it is also important to note the "teaching" roles played by fluent speakers of the language. The evidence accumulated so far suggests that young children are inconsistent as teachers of each other. Sometimes they are willing to make adjustments for second language learners, slowing, simplifying, repeating, and enunciating their speech carefully to assist the second language learner. At other times they lose patience with the task and carry on with their own agendas (Peck, 1977; Fillmore, 1976). However, a recent study has demonstrated that English speaking preschool children may be trained to interact effectively with their non-English speaking peers in ways that facilitate second language development (Hirschler, 1991). In general, however, adults are better and more consistent language teachers, both because they are willing to engage in language modifications for second language learners similar to those documented for caregivers in the native language, and because they are more willing to go to great lengths to sustain interactions with children, working both to understand and to be understood and checking frequently on children's comprehension (Tabors, 1987; Urzua, 1989; Hudelson, 1990). All of this suggests that second language acquisition is more similar to first language acquisition than it is different and that caring adults have an important role to play in children's second language development.

How Young Children Become
Readers and Writers

Up to this point this I have focused on children becoming users of oral language. Now I want to consider questions of how children become readers and writers, how children acquire written language, to examine what many have termed the *emergence of children's literacy* (Goodman, 1980; Sulzby, 1991; Teale & Sulzby, 1986). For at least the last fifteen years, it has become increasingly clear that children in print-saturated or print-oriented societies are engaged, from very early in their lives, in making sense of the printed word, in figuring out the symbolic nature of print, in discovering that print may serve a variety of functions (Taylor, 1983). Children also are engaged in experimenting with that print, whether they are interpreting print written by someone else (reading) or creating their own written texts (writing). So the notion of creative construction also applies to children's construction of written language. And this creative construction takes place within a variety of social interactions.

Demonstrations of and
Purposes for Literacy

One of the first contexts or social settings for many children's grappling with the meaning and function of print is the text in the world around them, including print in children's communities and homes and print on television. This kind of written language demonstration has come to be termed *environmental print*. Work with preschoolers (Baghban, 1984; Goodman & Altwerger, 1981; Harste, Woodward, & Burke, 1984) has demonstrated that children even younger than three years old are able to identify such familiar signs as McDonald's and STOP and such product labels as Coca-Cola and Crest. The most important reality, in terms of children constructing their understandings of written language, is the realization of the symbolic nature of the written language, that the label stands for something else. Early awareness of and interaction with environmental print occur across socioeconomic classes (Harste, Woodward, & Burke, 1984; Taylor & Dorsey-Gaines,

1988). Such awareness and interaction also occur among children whose native language is not English, as illustrated by the work of respected early childhood literacy researcher Yetta Goodman (Goodman, Goodman, & Flores, 1979). Goodman discovered that even young non-English speaking Navajo children living in remote parts of the Navajo Nation can identify some English print from the environment and the names of cartoon characters such as Spider Man.

Investigations into children's knowledge of environmental print extended into work documenting home literacy environments and experiences of preschool learners. Based on the understanding that literacy begins in the home, this work has examined both varieties of written language and the kinds of home literacy events observed by and often engaged in by preschool children. In a fascinating case study of a single child's language and literacy development from birth to age three, for example, Baghban (1984) noted striking parallels in her daughter Giti's oral and written language development. As Giti learned to talk by using speech to meet her needs and by engaging in talk with her parents and others around her, so she began to become literate as she observed her parents reading and writing for various reasons and as she engaged in writing and reading along with them. Baghban provides examples of Giti engaging, between the ages of one and a half and three, in letter and list writing with the two kinds of scribble writing taking the actual physical forms of letters and grocery lists. Baghban also provides transcripts of Giti engaged with an adult in repeated readings of favorite stories. Baghban demonstrates that as her daughter's speech became more complete, so did her renditions of the stories. Giti began her participation in storybook reading by echoing what she heard read to her so that her babbling sounded as though she were reading in English. Giti moved from this to labeling the pictures and from there to using the overall plot to provide more complete renditions of stories.

While work done in middle-class settings such as Giti's (Baghban, 1984; Taylor, 1983) has made it clear that literacy is a salient feature of socioeconomically advantaged preschool children's lives, investigations carried out among families that represent a variety of cultural, linguistic, and socioeconomic backgrounds have proven that home literacy is not limited to the middle class (Anderson, Teale, & Estrada, 1980; Teale, 1986).

Returning to the Trackton and Roadville families, Heath examined written as well as oral language use in these two communities and contrasted them to each other and to the Townspeople. She found multiple literacy types and uses in all settings. Heath's categories were later used by Taylor and Dorsey-Gaines (1988) to compare studies of family literacy carried out among middle-class suburban Anglo families in the Northeast (Taylor, 1983) and Heath's Piedmont region familes to working-class African American families in an urban area, the Shay Avenue neighborhood, in the Northeast. Taylor and Dorsey-Gaines learned that in all these settings reading and writing served multiple purposes. Families engaged in:

> instrumental reading to gain information about and accomplish practical goals of daily life
> social-interactional reading to gain information pertinent to building and maintaining social relationships
> news-related reading to gain information about events in the world
> recreational-pleasure reading to spend leisure time and plan recreational events
> confirmational reading to check or confirm facts and/or beliefs
> critical-educational reading to increase one's knowledge.

Families also engaged in:

> writing that substituted or reinforced oral messages
> social-interactional writing to build and maintain relationships and fulfill obligations
> writing to aid one's memory
> financial writing to keep track of records
> public record writing
> expository writing designed to communicate information through extended prose.

Taylor and Dorsey-Gaines also discovered that families in the Shay Avenue neighborhood engaged in certain kinds of reading and writing not considered in the other studies, specifically:

> reading to explore one's personal and cultural identity
> reading to consider changes in one's economic life
> writing one's autobiography
> writing to meet one's daily life obligations
> writing to pass leisure time
> writing for personal expression
> writing related to employment.

Thus, in all these settings, preschool children saw multiple demonstrations of literacy.

I would be leaving you with an inaccurate impression of these studies, however, if I suggested that the literacy uses and types were identical in these families. In fact, there were significant differences in the numbers and types of various literacy events and in the conduct of the events themselves. Heath's analysis is particularly instructive in this regard, because she discovered (1983) that differences in the way literacy events were conducted in the homes often had significant effects on how children coped with the literacy practices of the schools. In Trackton, for example, there were many fewer children's books in people's homes than in Roadville or Townspeople. Townspeople children had multiple experiences with storybook reading and with answering what have been termed known answer or display questions about books (questions such as What's this story about? Who's in the story? What's happening in this picture?) Consequently, Trackton children entering school were less used to storybook reading as a literacy practice and less successful in participating in storybook reading because they were not used to answering the kind of known answer display questions teachers asked with regard to the books.

In Roadville, adults frequently read stories to children. However, adults did not engage children above the age of three in discussions and picture identification as they read the books. Rather the children were expected to sit silently during and after the story. The Roadville children also did not engage in the expected kind of verbal behavior in storybook reading groups in school. Teachers interviewed by Heath, most of whom were Townspeople, talked about both the Trackton and Roadville children as being unable to perform as they should.

In homes of non-English speaking recent immigrants to the United States evidence also is accumulating that families engage in a variety of literacy practices. These tend to be focused on daily life, survival, and communication with relatives that have been left in their native countries, rather than on literacy for pleasure or to pass one's leisure time, especially when leisure time does not exist for parents working multiple jobs. Given economic circumstances and limited availability of material in their native languages, story reading to children is limited, although older siblings may bring home books from school to share with brothers and sisters. Young children, as integral parts of families, observe and sometimes participate in these events (Allexsaht-Snider, 1991; Delgado-Gaitan & Trueba, 1991; Schiefflein & Cochran-Smith, 1984; Vasquez, 1991).

All of this research has made it clear (Sulzby, 1991) that nearly all families, regardless of socioeconomic status, ethnicity, or home language, demonstrate a range of literacy events. By virtue of observing and participating in them preschool children come to understand some of the functions or purposes of literacy. However, one of the issues raised when children enter the public schools is whether the kinds of literacy events that children observe and participate in at home are similar to school literacy practices. In many cases, as we have seen, these events are quite different, and children often experience difficulty with what schools expect in terms of literacy concepts and participation in literacy events (Au, 1993).

Storybook Reading/Storytelling

Storybook reading, one literacy event both highly valued by schools and found to be a predictor of later school success in reading (Wells, 1986), is a literacy experience in which many preschool children participate, as work previously mentioned has noted. Numerous studies of preschool storybook reading have been conducted, most of them involving reading in which an adult or older fluent reader reads the same story multiple times to and with a child. This research has shown that, in spite of significant differences in how the reading is conducted, through storybook reading young children come to understand how stories are structured and the specific language used in stories (Baghban, 1984; Doake, 1985; Teale & Sulzby, 1986; Teale & Sulzby, 1989). They also come to understand that both the illustrations and the print are significant; that the illustrations help convey the story's meaning; and that the print (the squiggles on the page) represents the language of the story. They come to understand how to handle books, what the parts of a book are, and the concept of directionality both for a whole book and for print on a page (Clay, 1985).

Children's hypotheses about how to read a familiar story change over time (Weaver, 1988). Children begin more globally by constructing the overall plot and using the pictures to provide a general reconstruction of the story. As the story becomes more familiar, children focus in on the story's actual words, the story's sentences and vocabulary. Children begin to give more attention to the actual text of the story and attend to syntactic and semantic aspects of it. As children pay more attention to the actual words, they also begin to try to match the words they are saying to the squiggles on the page. Thus they cue in on individual words and letters. There is a natural process of reading acquisition, then, which moves from whole to part, with children beginning with global notions of what reading is and gradually refining their notions (Weaver, 1988). It appears that, in terms of storybooks, children begin with the whole story and gradually work their way down to the parts.

The social context for this acquisition is the joint collaborative effort of reading and constructing stories engaged in by adult and child or children. As in adult-child jointness in talking, the more proficient reader's demonstration of reading, including the work of predicting and inferencing, the response to and encouragement of the child's reading efforts, the assistance provided the young reader when necessary, all contribute to the child's continued efforts and ever more close approximations to adult reading behavior (Doake, 1985; Philips & McNaughton, 1990; Snow & Goldfield, 1982).

. In addition to work done with native English speakers, we also have evidence that reading emerges gradually as children are read to and engage in reading themselves both in languages other than English and among children for whom English is not the native language. Seawell (1985) has documented five- and six-year-old Spanish-English bilingual and English-as-a-second-language Mexican American children's construction of reading over a twelve-week period of sustained interactions with highly predictable books in both languages. Carger (1993) discovered that Spanish-speaking kindergarten children who engaged in what she called multiple "pretend" readings of the same picture book as part of their English as a second language time used more of the exact words of the story each time the story was reread and they then reread the story. Storybook reading contributed to these children's learning vocabulary in English.

In a research project whose data collection was concluded last spring, two colleagues and I have been documenting the Spanish language literacy development of primary school children enrolled in a bilingual program in Phoenix, Arizona. Many of these children at kindergarten entry had no previous schooling experiences and little experience with books. Our data collection included tape-recording the children as they read both familiar and unfamiliar children's books. Analyzing the kindergarten children's data, we have seen their renditions of familiar stories change over time. In the first tapings, the children reconstructed the stories using the illustrations and their recollections of the language of the author. The children did not tend to focus on the print in the stories. There was neither pointing to particular lines as they read nor voice-print match. In fact one of the children, who reconstructed an entire story from memory, told us proudly, "Yo puedo leer sin ver" (I can read without looking). Gradually, with familiar books, the children attended more to the actual print, attempting to match the words that they said to the words on the pages and even commenting on individual letters within words (Serna & Hudelson, 1993). Thus, children learned to read by being read to and by reading themselves.

Response to Literature

In addition to work with children's emergence as readers through participation in reading, there is also work being done on young children's response to literature. Susan Lehr's research (1991), which has explored children's construction or interpretation of stories (the why the author wrote this story issue) stands out in this area. Working with each child in her study individually, Lehr read Pat Hutchins' story *Titch* (1971). She then interviewed each child and later asked each child to respond positively or negatively to a list of possible themes for the book. Lehr found that, while the children were not able to generate theme statements, they were able to talk about thematic elements. They were also able to talk about the motivation of the characters and relate the book to their own life experiences. When given possible theme statements, the children chose one or more statements and explained their choices. There was diversity of opinion on the theme, suggesting that children interpreted the story differently, according to their own individual experiences. This idea of multiple interpretations is one that is supported by many researchers and practitioners who view reading as a transaction between the reader and the text (Rosenblatt, 1938) and who suggest that multiple interpretations are inevitable. Another source for appreciating children's interpretations of stories is Vivian Paley's *Wally's Stories* (1981), which contains numerous examples of children's responses to books and stories read and told in their kindergarten classroom.

Before finishing my summary of language acquisition research with reference to preschool children's writing development, I think it is important to return to storytelling, which was considered in terms of oral language, and to acknowledge it as a kind of literate behavior. Particularly in culturally and linguistically diverse homes, there is evidence that oral storytelling is a tradition, that oral storytelling is a valued ability, and that preschool children both listen to and participate in oral storytelling. Moreover, the evidence indicates that this storytelling, sometimes carried out independently and sometimes jointly, gives young children a schema for how stories are put together and can serve as a basis for classroom reading (Au & Kawakami, 1985; Delgado-Gaitan & Trueba, 1991; Dyson, 1992; Vasquez, 1991). In my own research, for example, one of our case study kindergarten children, Juan, spent a large part of the spring of his kindergarten year creating a fanciful and well-developed story about three imaginary bears ("los osos malos") who came after him. Juan's story was much more complex and well developed than the stories of most of his classmates, and we wondered why. His mother shared with us that she told her children stories every night as she prepared dinner. After she told a story, the children told their own stories. This helped explain his storytelling ability.

Preschool Children's Writing Development

A final context for appreciating children's working to understand and construct written language comes from an examination of early childhood writing. It is clear that children begin to experiment with writing long before they receive formal instruction in writing and long before they express their purposes using the conventional symbols that adults use (Clay, 1975). We know that children's experimentation comes because they see demonstrations of writing all around them. As they watch others, they come to understand both that writing serves multiple functions and that writing is accomplished using particular symbols (Galda, Cullinan, & Strickland, 1993). Much earlier than age three, children may use scribbles similar to cursive writing to represent labels, names, or ideas. Over time, these scribbles come more closely to resemble adult writing. By the age of three many children already have distinguished between drawing and writing as two different symbol systems for expressing their meaning (Baghban, 1984; Weaver, 1988). Early letter forms children produce, whether in strings or in certain combinations, resemble the letters or symbols of the orthographic system that surrounds them, although they do not realize these forms have a specific relationship to sounds or concepts in the language (Ferreiro, 1990; Weaver, 1988).

While some may dismiss these efforts as children simply playing around or copying those around them, what they really indicate is learners struggling to figure out how the written language works. Young children are active constructors of the written language, and their representations of written language reflect their concepts, at any point in time, about how the language is structured. As their ideas or hypotheses change, so do the texts that they produce.

For many researchers, significant changes in children's writing occur when they figure out that the squiggles or forms in some way represent the sounds or words of the language they are writing. At this point in alphabetic languages such as English, children begin to relate the letters they are writing to the words they are creating and use invented spellings. Studies of invented spelling have made it clear that children's attempts at orthography are logical and reasoned, although they do not conform to conventional adult forms (Chomsky, 1971; Hudelson, 1981–82; Read, 1975). Moreover, invented spellings change over time. Consider, for example, the difference between the message: RCRBKD—our car broke down; and A KCID SOD A RAD AND PEC HWS—a kid sawed a red and pink house. In the first example, the child has represented each word by one or two letters, and segmentation between words has not appeared. In the second example, the young writer is representing words with more than one sound per word, using some vowels as well as consonants, using some phonetic features of sounds, and figuring out some spellings from a strategy of using letter names (Weaver, 1988). These examples demonstrate that, as children figure out the orthography of English, they use different strategies and patterns, using what they know about written English at any one time to generate, try out, and change their hypotheses. As children work to create meaning, they construct for themselves the orthographic rules of English.

Work on children's construction of written language also has taken place in languages other than English. Perhaps the best known research is that of Emilia Ferreiro and Ana Teberosky (1982) who investigated young Spanish-speaking children's development as writers in Spanish. They found that, long before they begin to use the alphabetic principle, children develop theories about how written language works. Using a limited number of letter forms, not real letters, children can express meaning by:

1. using different forms for different words
2. changing one or two forms in a sequence to create a different word
3. changing the order of the forms to create a different word.

Similarly, preschool children growing up in cultures where different systems are used, for example, Hebrew, Arabic, and Chinese, begin to create texts that resemble the written language of their cultures (Harste, Burke, & Woodward, 1984), exhibiting patterns of development similar to those described above (Landsmann, 1990; Lee, 1990).

The work just discussed, I believe, confirms that children, as they become literate, are creative constructors of their language. As they did with oral language, children engage in hypothesis creation and testing as they figure out how the written language works. The creative construction takes place within environments in which social interaction provides children both with demonstrations of how people use written language and opportunities to engage in written language use.

Conclusions and Challenges

In this chapter, I have tried to provide an overview of preschool children's language learning and use, including both oral and written language. Given available information, it seems to me that the following generalizations can be made:

1. Preschool children are active constructors of language, be it oral or written language. Children learn language and figure out how oral and written language function by observing other language users, by using language within their daily lives, and by engaging with others through the medium of language. Children come to understand both functions and forms of language through use.

2. Language learning is both social and cognitive—social in that learning requires engagement with others in a multiplicity of settings, and cognitive in that children figure out language by using available language data to create, test, and modify their hypotheses about how to say, read, or write something.
3. Home and community are crucial contexts for language learning and use. Children's early language learning occurs in the home and community, where children encounter demonstrations of how speech, reading, and writing are used, and where they involve themselves in using language in order to participate in home and community life.
4. There is significant variation in the ways in which families and communities use oral and written language, in the ways that family and community members participate in speech events, in the functions and types of reading and writing that occur, in the frequency of occurrence and the value placed on certain kinds of activities. Some communities' "ways with words" (Heath, 1983) are more congruent with the schools' expectations for oral and written language use and participation in classroom activities than those of other communities.
5. Families and communities represent multiple varieties of English as well as multiple languages. Children come to school and other settings using their home and community dialects and languages. Very often these varieties are not considered appropriate within the context of the schools.
6. By age five virtually all children have well developed, sophisticated speech abilities that reflect their home and/ or community norms. They also have understandings of some of the functions and types of literacy. Some children's abilities, concepts, understandings, and experiences with written language (for example, storybook reading) are a closer match to the expectations of schools and other institutions than are other children's.

Library Implications

Given these realities, it seems appropriate to conclude this chapter by thinking about possible implications of this information for our work in designing library programs and services for all preschool children. If our aim is to assure that all children will want to be a part of and will benefit from what we organize, I would like to challenge us all to keep in mind the following points, which, though familiar sounding, can be lost in the distractions of the workday:

1. We need to acknowledge that preschool children already know a tremendous amount of and about oral and written language, and we need to recognize that their knowledge and abilities keep increasing as they use language constantly in their daily lives. We need to see language learning as in constant flux and consider ways that we may contribute to that learning.
2. We need to understand and respect the ways in which children's understandings of and abilities with oral and written language develop in home and community settings and capitalize on those ways of knowing and learning.
3. We need to value diversity in English and include materials that reflect this diversity in terms of dialect features, oral traditions and folklore, storytelling, and literature that reflects multiple races, cultures, socioeconomic realities, and so on.
4. We need to value languages other than English and promote inclusion and utilization of materials in multiple languages that also reflect multiple dialects and genres.
5. We may need to adjust our ways of organizing, structuring, and implementing activities to allow for diverse interactional styles of children. That is, we may need to make what we do more culturally responsive to the members of our communities.

Meeting these challenges will, I believe, help assure that all children are well served by libraries that are concerned with helping young learners achieve their potentials.

Works Cited

Allexsaht-Snider, M. (1991). Family literacy in a Spanish speaking context: Joint construction of meaning. *The Quarterly News-*

letter of the Laboratory of Comparative Human Cognition, 13, (1), 15–21.

Anderson, A., Teale, W., & Estrada, I. (1980). Low-Income children's preschool literacy experiences. *The Quarterly Newsletter of the Laboratory of Comparative Human Cognition, 2* (3), 59–65.

Au, K. (1993). *Literacy instruction in multicultural settings.* Fort Worth, TX: Harcourt, Brace, Jovanovich.

Au, K., & Kawakami, A. (1985). Research currents: Talk story and learning to read. *Language Arts, 62* (4), 106–11.

Baghban, M. (1984). *Our daughter learns to read and write.* Newark, DE: International Reading Association.

Campbell, R., & Lindfors, J. (1969). *Insights into English structure: A programmed course.* Englewood Cliffs, NJ: Prentice-Hall.

Carger, C. (1993). Louie comes to life: Pretend reading with second language emergent readers. *Language Arts, 70* (7), 542–47.

Cazden, C. (1988). *Classroom discourse: the language of teaching and learning.* Portsmouth, NH: Heinemann.

Cazden, C., John, V., & Hymes, D. (1972). *The functions of language in the classroom.* New York: Teachers College Press.

Chaika, E. (1982). *Language: the social mirror* (2nd ed.). Rowley, MA: Newbury House.

Chomsky, C. (1971). Write first, read later. *Childhood Education, 47,* 296–301.

Clark, E. (1983). Meanings and concepts. In J. Flavell and E. Markman (Eds.), *Cognitive Development* (Vol. 3). New York: Wiley.

Clay, M. (1985). *The early detection of reading difficulties.* Portsmouth, NH: Heinemann.

Clay, M. (1975). *What did I write?* Auckland: Heinemann.

Clifton, L. (1973). *All us come cross the water.* New York: Holt, Rinehart & Winston.

Delpit, L. (1990). Language diversity and learning. In S. Hynds and D. Rubin (Eds.), *Perspectives on talk and learning.* Urbana, IL: National Council of Teachers of English.

Delgado-Gaitan, C., & Trueba, H. (1991). *Crossing cultural borders: Education for immigrant families in America.* Philadelphia, PA: Falmer.

Doake, D. (1985). Reading-like behavior: Its role in learning to read. In A. Jagger and M. Trika Smith-Burke (Eds.), *Observing the language learner.* Newark, DE: International Reading Association.

Dyson, A. (1992). Children's place in the language arts curriculum: Victims, beneficiaries, and critics. *English Education,* 3–19.

Ferreiro, E. (1990). Literacy development: Psychogenesis. In Y. Goodman (Ed.), *How children construct literacy: Piagetian perspectives.* Newark, DE: International Reading Association.

Ferreiro, E., & Teberosky, A. (1982). *Literacy before schooling.* Exeter, NH: Heinemann.

Fillmore, L.W. (1976). *The second time around: Cognitive and social strategies in second language acquisition.* Unpublished doctoral dissertation, Stanford University, Palo Alto, CA.

Fillmore, L.W. (1991). When learning a second language means losing the first. *Early Childhood Research Quarterly,* 6 (3), 323–346.

Fishman, J., Cooper, R. L., & Ma, R. (1971). *Bilingualism in the barrio.* Bloomington, IN: Research Center in Anthropology, Folklore and Linguistics, Indiana University.

Galda, L., Cullinan, B., & Strickland, D. (1993). *Language, literacy and the child.* Fort Worth, TX: Harcourt, Brace, Jovanovich.

Genishi, C., & Dyson, A. (1984). *Language assessment in the early years.* Norwood, NJ: Ablex.

Goodman, K., Goodman, Y., & Flores, B. (1979). *Reading in the bilingual classroom: Literacy and biliteracy.* Rosslyn, VA: National Clearinghouse for Bilingual Education.

Goodman, Y. (1980). The roots of literacy. In M. Douglass (Ed.), *Claremont Reading Conference, 44th Yearbook.* Claremont, CA: Claremont Reading Conference.

Goodman, Y., & Altwerger, B. (1981). *Print awareness in pre-school children: A working paper.* Program in Language and Literacy, College of Education, University of Arizona, Tucson.

Harste, J., Burke, C., & Woodward, V. (1984). *Language stories and literacy lessons.* Exeter, NH: Heinemann.

Heath, S. (1983). *Ways with words.* New York: Cambridge University Press.

Hirschler, J. (1991). *Preschool children's help to second language learners.* Unpublished doctoral dissertation, Harvard University, Cambridge, MA.

Hudelson, S. (1990). Bilingual/ESL learners in the English classroom. In S. Hynds & D. Rubin (Eds.), *Perspectives on talk and learning.* Urbana, IL: National Council of Teachers of English.

Hudelson, S. (1981–82). An introductory examination of children's invented spelling in Spanish. *National Association for Bilingual Education Journal, VI,* 53–68.

Hutchins, P. (1971). *Titch.* New York: Macmillan.

Hymes, D. (1974). *Foundations in sociolinguistics: An ethnographic approach.* Philadelphia, PA: University of Pennsylvania Press.

Johnson, D. (1994). Grouping strategies for second language learners. In F. Genesee (Ed.), *Educating second language children: The whole child, the whole curriculum, the whole community.* New York, NY: Cambridge University Press.

Labov, W. (1970). The logic of nonstandard English. In F. Williams (Ed.), *The Language of Poverty.* Chicago, IL: Marxham.

Landsmann, L.T. (1990). Literacy development and pedagogical implications: Evidence from the Hebrew system of writing. In Y. Goodman (Ed.), *How children construct literacy: Piagetian perspectives.* Newark, DE: International Reading Association.

Lee, L. (1990). *Developing control of reading and writing in Chinese.* Program in Language and Literacy, Division of Language, Literacy and Culture, College of Education, University of Arizona, Tucson.

Lehr, S. (1991). *The child's developing sense of theme.* New York, NY: Teacher's College Press.

Lindfors, J. (1990). Speaking creatures in the classroom. In S. Hynds & D. Rubin (Eds.), *Perspectives on talk and learning.* Urbana, IL: National Council of Teachers of English.

Lindfors, J. (1987). *Children's language and learning.* 2nd ed. Englewood Cliffs, NJ: Prentice-Hall.

Michaels, S. (1981). 'Sharing time': Children's narrative styles and differential access to literacy. *Language in Society, 10* (3), 423–42.

Michaels, S. (1986). Narrative presentations: an oral preparation for literacy. In J. Cook-Gumperz (Ed.), *The social construction of literacy.* Cambridge, MA: Harvard University Press.

Paley, V. (1981). *Wally's stories: Conversations in the kindergarten.* Cambridge, MA: Harvard University Press.

Peck, S. (1977). Child-child discourse in second language acquisition. In E. Hatch (Ed.), *Second language acquisition* (pp. 383–400). Rowley, MA: Newbury House.

Philips, S. (1983). *The invisible culture.* New York, NY: Longmans.

Phillips, G., & McNaughton, S. (1990). The practice of storybook reading to preschoolers in mainstream New Zealand families. *Reading Research Quarterly, 25,* 196–212.

Ramirez, D., Yuen, S., & Ramel, D. (1991). *Executive summary: Longitudinal study of structured English immersion, early-exit, and late-exit transitional bilingual education programs for language minority children.* San Mateo, CA: Aguirre International.

Read, C. (1975). *Children's categorization of speech sounds in English.* Urbana, IL: National Council of Teachers of English.

Rosenblatt, L. (1938). *The reader, the text, the poem: The transactional theory of the literary work.* Carbondale, IL: Southern Illinois University Press.

Schiefflein, B. & Cochran-Smith, M. (1984). Learning to read culturally: Literacy before schooling. In H. Goelman, A. Oberg & F. Smith (Eds.), *Awakening to literacy.* Exeter, NH: Heinemann.

Seawell, R. P. M. (1985). *A micro-ethnographic study of a Spanish-English bilingual kindergarten in which literature and puppet play were used as a method of enhancing language growth.* Unpublished doctoral dissertation, University of Texas, Austin.

Serna, I., & Hudelson, S. (1993). Emergent Spanish literacy in a whole language bilingual program. In R. Donmoyer & R. Kos (Eds.), *At-risk students: Portraits, programs and practices.* Albany, NY: SUNY Albany Press.

Smitherman, G. (1977). *Talkin and testifyin.* Boston, MA: Houghton Mifflin.

Snow, C. & Goldfield, A. (1982). Building stories: The emergence of information structures from conversations. In D. Tannen (Ed.),

Analyzing discourse: Text and talk. Washington, DC: Georgetown University Press.

Sulzby, E. (1991). The development of the young child and the emergence of literacy. In J. Flood, J. Jensen, D. Lapp, & J. Squires (Eds.), *Handbook of research on teaching the English language arts.* New York: Macmillan.

Tabors, P. (1987). *The development of communicative competence by second language learners in a nursery school classroom: An ethnolinguistic study.* Unpublished doctoral dissertation, Harvard University, Cambridge, MA.

Tabors, P. & Snow, C. (1994). English as a second language in preschool programs. In F. Genesee (Ed.), *Educating second language children: The whole child, the whole curriculum, the whole community.* New York, NY: Cambridge University Press.

Tannen, D. (1984). *Conversational style: Analyzing talk among friends.* Norwood, NJ: Ablex.

Taylor, D. (1983). *Family literacy: Young children learn to read and write.* Portsmouth, NH: Heinemann.

Taylor, D., & Dorsey-Gaines, C. (1988). *Growing up literate: Learning from inner-city families.* Portsmouth, NH: Heinemann.

Teale, W., & Sulzby, E. (1986). Emergent literacy as a perspective for examining how young children become writers and readers. In W. Teale & E. Sulzby (Eds.), *Emergent literacy: Writing and reading.* Norwood, NJ: Ablex.

Teale, W., & Sulzby, E. (1989). Emergent literacy: New perspectives on young children's reading and writing. In D.S. Strickland & L. M. Morrow (Eds.), *Emerging literacy: Young children learn to read and write.* Newark, DE: International Reading Association.

Urzua, C. (1989). I grow for a living. In P. Rigg & V. Allen (Eds.), *When they don't all speak English.* Urbana, IL: National Council of Teachers of English.

Vasquez, O. (1991). Reading the world in a multicultural setting: A Mexicano perspective. *Quarterly Newsletter of the Laboratory of Comparative Human Cognition, 13,* 13–15.

Waggoner, D. (1992). The increasing multiethnic and multilingual diversity of the U.S.: Findings from the 1990 census. *TESOL Matters,* October/November 1992. 12–13.

Weaver, C. (1988). *Reading: Process and practice.* Portsmouth, NH: Heinemann.

Wells, G. (1986). *The meaning makers: Children learning language and using language to learn.* Portsmouth, NH: Heinemann.

Wells, G. (1985). *Language development in the pre-school years.* Cambridge, MA: Harvard University Press.

Williams, F. (1980). *Language and poverty.* Chicago, IL: Marxham.

CHAPTER 6

Public Libraries and Emergent Literacy
Helping Set the Foundation for School Success

WILLIAM H. TEALE

The issue of children's cognitive readiness for school is a centrally important one for librarians and early childhood educators. What children know, their strategies for thinking and problem solving, and their attitudes toward learning are pivotal to eventual academic success in school and to their overall views of themselves as learners in the world. In discussing the topic of cognitive readiness for school, I have chosen to focus on young children's literacy and language learning. This focus was selected for two reasons. First, no area is as central to a child's overall success in school as literacy. The ability to read and write is fundamental to achievement in virtually all school subjects. Second, above all, librarians are concerned with children's interactions with the written word and can play a key role in enhancing children's love of and learning from written language.

Over the past fifteen years, ideas about young children's learning and development have changed profoundly. In perhaps no area of cognitive development have the changes been

WILLIAM H. TEALE is professor, College of Education, University of Illinois at Chicago. With Elizabeth Sulzby, he edited *Emergent Literacy: Writing and Reading* in 1986. He is currently editor of *Language Arts*. He has extensive research experience in emergent literacy.

as marked as with views about early reading and writing. The traditional perspective—a concentration on reading readiness—began shifting at the end of the 1970s. By the mid-1980s, Teale and Sulzby (1986) had published an edited book of articles by researchers whose work paved the way for a transformation to emergent literacy, currently the generally accepted way of thinking about the reading and writing development of young children among researchers, early childhood educators, and librarians alike (Greene, 1991; Sulzby & Teale, 1991; Teale & Sulzby, 1989).

Emergent literacy changed our thinking about early reading and writing development in five especially important ways:

1. Instead of thinking that learning to read and write begins only after a set of prerequisite reading readiness skills has been mastered, we now believe that:

   Learning to read and write begins very early in life for almost all children in a literate society like ours.

2. Instead of thinking that children become proficient in oral language first and then learn to read and then learn to write, we now believe that:

   From the beginning, reading and writing develop concurrently and interrelatedly rather than sequentially.

3. Instead of thinking that reading and writing are learned by young children as a series of abstract, separate skills in a decontextualized fashion, we now believe that:

   The meaningful/functional/purposeful bases of early literacy are a critically important part of learning to read and write, and must be emphasized so that children learn strategies within such contexts, not in isolation.

4. Instead of thinking that skill in visual and auditory discrimination and knowledge of letters and sounds are the essence of what young children need to learn about literacy, we now believe that:

   A much broader range of knowledge, dispositions, and strategies is involved in young children's becom-

ing literate. These include, among other things, the functions of language and literacy, knowledge of stories and how they work, understanding the nature of written language, and concepts about print, as well as phonemic awareness and knowledge of letters and sound-symbol relationships.

5. Instead of thinking that children follow the same skills path into reading and writing, we now believe that:

   Children become literate at different rates and take a variety of different paths to conventional reading and writing.

Thus, we currently have a different perspective on the importance of the early years for literacy learning, and our notions of what children are learning and how they are learning have changed significantly also. These understandings have caused many librarians, child care professionals, and early childhood teachers to rethink their programs and curricula. One need only read early childhood or reading education journals, note the trends in family literacy programs (see, for example, Goldsmith, 1993; Goldsmith & Handel, 1990; or Quezada & Nickse, 1993), or look to projects like the Head Start–Library Partnership Program, Born to Read, and library-based family literacy programs (see, for example, Monsour & Talan, 1993, or the Cargill Project) to realize that early childhood in general and early childhood literacy learning in particular have been rediscovered. In the remainder of this chapter, I discuss ways that librarians can promote emergent literacy and issues to be considered in those efforts, as well as examine some of the many exciting initiatives that are currently taking place in the name of emergent literacy in libraries across the United States.

What Can Libraries and Librarians Do to Promote Emergent Literacy?

General Principles

I see two general ways in which libraries and librarians can make significant contributions to the emergent literacy development of young children in the United States. One is to work cooperatively with family literacy programs or other community-wide programs that serve children in their homes or in community locations. Library involvement in such programs can run the gamut from providing information, such as recommended storybook reading lists, to full partnerships with a range of other institutions that work with families and children. Examples of community-based early childhood literacy projects involving public libraries include "Read All About It . . . Together," the ALA–Cargill Project, and many of the Massachusetts Community Collaboration for Family Literacy projects.

The second way libraries can promote early literacy learning is through special programs that the library itself runs. Such programs may actually take place in the library (e.g., story time), or the library may distribute materials that are used in homes or facilities such as child care centers (e.g., Beginning with Books [Segel & Friedberg, 1991] or Project LEAP [Rome, 1989]). Another possibility is that the library may take the program into the community, as do Project BEACON (The Carnegie Library of Pittsburgh) or Stories to Go (Rowan Public Library, Rowan County, North Carolina [Lytle, 1994]), to name just two.

Both of these general ways that libraries and librarians work to promote literacy development in preschool children have proved effective. It remains for the individual library to examine the range of existing programs, add its own vision to the possibilities, and decide what it can do in light of available resources and personnel. The range of possibilities seems to expand each month as more and more public libraries find creative ways of enhancing preschoolers' reading and writing development. There is no one source that summarizes all the different projects that exist. However, both *Books, Babies, and Libraries: Serving Infants, Toddlers, Their Parents and Caregivers* (Greene, 1991) and *Library-Based Family Literacy Projects* (Monsour & Talan, 1993) contain a number of good ideas and descriptions of quality programs. Whatever format a library chooses, there are specific facets of early literacy learning that it will be helpful for program directors and librarians to think about in planning to make the experiences provided for the children as rich as possible.

Promoting Emergent Literacy:
Specific Areas of Support

There are numerous areas of children's early literacy learning that can be developed through the thoughtful participation of libraries and librarians. I have chosen to highlight three: storybook reading, playing with language, and literacy and play. I have focused on these areas for two main reasons: they are compatible with the existing mission of most public libraries, and of all the things libraries might focus on, these areas are the ones that I believe will have the best payoff for the children. In other words, libraries will get the biggest bang for the buck by putting efforts into promoting storybook reading, language play, and literacy activities in the context of children's play.

STORYBOOK READING

Research dating back at least sixty years has shown that storybook reading is the single most important literacy experience children can have during their preschool years that affects their readiness for school and continued school achievement (Sulzby & Teale, 1991). I believe it is helpful to think of young children's storybook reading experience as consisting of two important dimensions: (1) being read to by an adult (parent or other family member, teacher, or librarian; and (2) "reading" on their own (called emergent storybook readings).

READING TO CHILDREN

Librarians are well acquainted with the fact that preschool storybook reading experience is positively correlated with the development of a wide range of language and literacy abilities in young children. Furthermore, it is very common for libraries to provide in-house storybook reading programs at the library or to run outreach programs aimed at families (e.g., Beginning with Books [Segel & Friedberg, 1991]); child care professionals or preschool teachers (e.g., Project LEAP in the Cuyahoga County [Ohio] Public Library [Rome, 1989]; Project BEACON in The Carnegie Library of Pittsburgh); or others in the community. Outreach projects typically seek to reach children directly through read-aloud programs or to educate parents, preschool teachers, or child care professionals in what and how to read to preschoolers.

I do not wish to dwell on a concept and activity that is well known to librarians. However, I should like to point out three major insights from recent research that are useful to think about as librarians bring their storybook reading programs to fruition or as storybook reading training programs for parents, child care personnel, or teachers are planned and implemented:

1. *It is the language and social interaction that surround the book during the reading, not merely the words and pictures of the book itself, that cause storybook reading to be so powerful an activity for young children.*

What the adult and child(ren) talk about before, during, and after the reading of the text has a profound influence on what children actually "get" from storybook reading. Furthermore, research has shown that parents and teachers actually have different "storybook reading styles" (Dickinson & Smith, 1994; Martinez & Teale, 1988; Sulzby & Teale, 1987) that appear to affect the ways children approach books, as well as what and how much they learn from being read to (Dickinson, Hao, & He, 1993; Heath, 1982; Ninio, 1980; Teale & Martinez, submitted for publication).

There is not space here to provide details about the different read-aloud styles that have been identified in research. Suffice to say that what is talked about, how it is talked about, and how much the world of the book is connected to the world of the child differs across readers, even when the text is the same. Several studies in this body of research further indicate that there are effects of the book-reading style on children's comprehension of and learning from text: different styles affect children differentially.

The idea of storybook reading style has important implications for getting people to reflect on the way in which they read to children and on the type of training in how to read to children that is presented. In other words, it's not just how much we read to children that is important, but also how. My recommendation is that people who run library training programs become familiar with the idea of storybook reading styles and their effects so that they can use the information to guide their training and help them reflect on the whole idea. Common suggestions about how to read aloud that are made in training programs include reading with expression, using character voices, and asking children open-ended questions. But beyond these general recommendations, the research literature suggests other reading style characteristics that are positively related to children's growth and to their enjoyment of storybook time:

- the dramatic quality of the reading and the level of adult engagement in the activity (Dickinson, Hao, & He, 1993)

- the text-to-life connections the adult helps the children make (Heath, 1982)

- the amount of child-involved analytic talk (Dickinson & Smith, 1994)

- drawing children's attention to important, textually and pictorially explicit story information (Teale & Martinez, submitted for publication).

Furthermore, experience from programs focused on teaching child care providers and teachers how to read aloud to children (e.g., Sesame Street PEP Initiative [developed by Children's Television Workshop, New York]; Beginning with Books; Project BEACON) indicates that factors like the following are important:

- stopping the reading at key points and getting children to predict what they think will happen next

- talking with children about the author and illustrator of the book

- doing follow-up art, drama, or music activities that extend the storybook experience.

2. *The types of text that young children experience in storybook reading are important to consider.*

Narratives—stories—should be at the heart of storybook time. Story is somehow basic to what we are as human beings, as theorists like Barbara Hardy (1977) and Jerome Bruner (1990) and teachers like Vivian Paley (1981, 1984, 1990) have helped us understand. Thus, stories form the core of what we read aloud to children. Stories are important for the cultural "lessons" they offer children and for the important psychological structures such as *story grammar* (Mandler & Johnson, 1977) they help children develop. Moreover, steeping children in stories begins their appreciation of the craft of literature as well as the content. In short, narrative texts constitute the fundamental essence of books for preschoolers.

Another type of book commonly read during story time for preschoolers, especially if only one child or a very small number of children is being read to, is the concept book. These books, with simple text and straightforward illustrations that center on concepts such as colors, shapes, the names of common things or animals, and so forth, are especially important for helping young children develop the basic vocabulary and knowledge onto which they will build more complex vocabulary and thinking. Sometimes, also, these books have guessing-game formats like *Whose Baby?* (Yabuuchi, 1981) or predictable-language formats like *Brown Bear, Brown Bear, What Do You See?* (Martin, 1967) and thus are highly involving for children because of the interactive nature of the reading.

Both stories and concept books are enormously important for young children's language and literacy learning, but I would also like to encourage the reading of two other types of texts: poetry (including songs) and information (expository) books. Poetry is important because it offers a special aesthetic experience for children and because it is a powerful way of using language. In addition, rhyming poetry and songs have an added benefit for the literacy development of young children. Rhyming is the foundation for a child's development of phonemic awareness, the ability to hear the constituent sounds that make up words. The role and importance of phonemic awareness in learning to read are discussed in detail later in this chapter. Let us just say at this point that to be able to reflect on and manipulate the sounds of language is an important part of what all children who learn to read an alphabetic written language like English or Spanish must do—become efficient at decoding printed words. Learning how sound-symbol relations work actually begins in rhyming, as children become used to taking words apart and putting them back together again. Thus, poetry can serve several purposes as part of the regular read-aloud diet; its significance cannot be stressed too much.

Information books are important because children need to learn how expository texts work. As children move into the upper elementary grades and middle school, the types of texts they have to read in school become increasingly expository. Expository text is different from narrative in its structures and the demands it places on readers for comprehension. Furthermore, research suggests that one of the reasons for the phenomenon known as the "fourth grade slump" (increasing numbers of children begin falling even further behind in reading in the upper elementary grades and on into middle school) is the difficulties children experience in processing expository texts (Chall, Jacobs, & Baldwin, 1990).

Becoming familiar with the language and organizational structures of expository text is a process that can begin in early childhood. We now have increasing numbers of high-quality information books that are appropriate for preschool children. For example, Ann Morris and Ken Heyman have teamed to produce several excellent informational books for young children, of which *Bread, Bread, Bread* (Morris, 1989) is but one example. Simple pop-up books like *Frogs* (Tarrant, 1983), one in a series titled Natural Pop-Ups, depict and explain the life cycles of particular animals. Hanna Machotka has produced a number of books like *Breathtaking Noses* (Machotka, 1992) that combine both expository text interesting to young children and a guessing-game format. With this increasing number of high-quality expository trade books for young children, there is every reason to incorporate them into what we read aloud during storybook time.

Before concluding this discussion of the types of texts I feel young children should experience in story time, I want to point out that I have not gone into the issue of making multicultural books an everyday part of what we read to young children. Doing so is of critical importance to educating our next generation to live well and productively with each other.

In fact, I believe there is no more important agenda for all of our education institutions than educating for diversity in our society. The reason I have not addressed in detail the need for multicultural books to be a routine part of storybook time is not that it is not significant; it is that I believe this is a point that should be well known to librarians. In the last few years numerous books (e.g., *Against Borders* [Rochman, 1993]; *The Multicolored Mirror* [Cooperative Children's Book Center, M. V. Lindgren, Ed., 1991]; *Our Family, Our Friends, Our World* [Miller-Lachmann, 1992]; *Teaching Multicultural Literature in Grades K-8* [Harris, 1992]); articles in professional journals (e.g., Sims Bishop's "Books from Parallel Cultures" column in *Horn Book* or Yokota, 1993); and other materials have served to make the community who work with children and books aware of the central role that multicultural books have in providing services to customers, young and old alike. We have not yet succeeded in making multicultural books the everyday experience they should be for preschool children, but making sure such literature is a regular part of what we read aloud is one way of doing so.

3. *Repeated readings of certain books are extremely important for young children.*

There is a myriad of excellent quality children's books available to us today, and naturally we want to expose children to as many of these books as possible. But it is equally important for children to visit some books repeatedly. Research shows that the storybook reading experience changes with repeated readings; in other words, children actually get something new each time they experience the story (Snow & Ninio, 1986; Teale & Sulzby, 1987). Also, repeated opportunities to experience a text enable the child to "read" the text by herself or himself, which, as we shall see in the following section of this chapter, is an important part of a young child's early literacy learning. Finally, as Hudelson (Chapter Five) points out, repeated readings of books are very important to the language and literacy development of children acquiring English as a second or third language. Therefore, in library storybook reading programs, we should make provisions to read certain books over and over; in training others to read aloud, we should stress the importance of repeated readings.

Predictable books (books with repetitive structures and/or patterned language) are especially suited to repeated readings because children soon pick up on the predictability of the plot and language and are actually able to join in on the reading after a time or two. Examples of these are *The Chick and the Ducking* (Ginsburg, 1972), *The Napping House* (Wood, 1984), *Brown Bear, Brown Bear, What Do You See?* (Martin, 1967). Also, evidence suggests that children will "read" (emergently) predictable books on their own more often than nonpredictable ones (Martinez & Teale, 1988; Teale, Martinez, & McKeown, 1994). However, it is also good to read repeatedly other kinds of books besides predictable books.

YOUNG CHILDREN READING ON THEIR OWN: EMERGENT STORYBOOK READING

The other important dimension of storybook reading is that young children have opportunities to "read" books on their own. These types of interactions with books are frequently called "pretend readings"; researchers commonly refer to them as *emergent storybook readings* because the children are reading in not-yet-conventional ways. Emergent storybook readings occur with books that have been read repeatedly to the children. With these familiar books, children may attend to the illustrations in the book and tell the story or even use a very reading-like intonation to deliver an almost verbatim account of the text. Several research studies have shown that these emergent storybook reading behaviors play an important role in becoming literate (Sulzby, 1985; Sulzby & Teale, 1987). Furthermore, there appears to be a developmental character to young children's emergent storybook reading that reflects children's growing reading knowledge and strategies.

Sulzby's (1985) original research into the phenomenon of emergent storybook readings showed eleven different categories of emergent storybook reading strategies that preschoolers exhibited. Such a categorization scheme is too fine-grained for use by librarians or classroom teachers. The following simplification of Sulzby's research tool depicts the major storybook reading concepts and strategies that preschoolers exhibit:

What the Child is Reading	*What the Child is Doing*
1. Pictures	Labels, comments, and/or follows the action—no story formed
2. Pictures	Sounds like telling a story
3. Pictures	Part sounds like telling a story, part sounds like reading a story
4. Pictures	Sounds like reading a story
5. Print	Child may read sight words, track print with finger, and reconstruct the story from memory, or try to "sound out" words

Note that all of these ways of reading occur before the child is reading conventionally ("really reading" the print and comprehending the message). Children progress from focusing on various things or actions on the page ("There's a snowflake" or "She's jumping") with no connections among the pages (i.e., no story), to telling a story from the pictures, to reading from the pictures with a reading-like intonation, to beginning to focus on the print itself. These different types of behaviors show us children's growing knowledge of what they think it means to read a story and give us insight into what children are learning and what we can do to help them progress even more.

Implications of Storybook Reading Research for Librarians

Libraries are in a very strong position to promote quality storybook reading for young children. Of course, most libraries are already involved in this area. I see two especially promising ways that public libraries' current efforts in storybook reading for preschool children can be enhanced. One is

to incorporate into programs the emergent literacy perspective insights about storybook reading that were just discussed.
This means:

1. Trying to insure that all of your story readers understand
    the importance of engaging children in conversations about
    books during reading and that they are aware of different
    storybook reading styles and their effects on children.
2. Trying to stimulate more emergent storybook readings
    among the children themselves: Read certain books re-
    peatedly; provide the children with access to copies of the
    books that were read to them; encourage the children to
    read to each other or to stuffed animals or puppets.
3. Monitoring programs to make sure that you are including
    a variety of text types in read alouds so that children have
    plenty of opportunities to experience poetry and exposi-
    tory text.

The second promising practice is reaching out to additional constituencies in efforts to promote storybook reading.
I have not seen any systematic, comprehensive studies of who
attends story reading programs in libraries, but my hunch is
that a large percentage of them comes from homes where they
are already read to. An important mission for the library with
respect to the first national education goal of having all children arrive at school with an academic background that en-
ables them to participate fully in school instruction from the
beginning, is to bring storybook reading to children who
would not otherwise get it. In this regard, libraries can:

1. Develop additional programs for, and links with, parents of
    "at risk" children.
2. Educate child care professionals in how and what to read.
3. Do more in the way of taking books to children in their
    home and community settings.

There is a great deal of exciting work in all of these areas
currently going on in America's public libraries, but it is not
yet enough. We need to expand currently successful storybook reading programs, we need to extend these successful

programs into more libraries, and we need to keep working to develop more innovative ways of connecting preschoolers with the magic of storybook reading in their homes and their libraries.

Playing with Language

Experiencing the joy of hearing and using language is something that helps entice children into becoming lifelong readers. One of our goals as we work with preschoolers should be to get them reveling in the sounds, cadences, and intonations of speech. We want them to enjoy playing with the sounds of language, reflecting on how sounds go together in different and interesting ways to make funny-sounding, or important-sounding, or sweet-sounding words. Such pleasure in language is an enormous motivational assistant in learning. Interestingly enough, research has also shown that the ability to reflect on and play with the sounds of language is closely connected with children's developing "basic skills" in decoding. A key concept that is useful for librarians to become acquainted with is *phonemic awareness.* Phonemic awareness refers to the ability to hear the constituent sounds (phonemes) that make up language.

One of the things young children learn about language is to break the stream of speech they hear into meaningful parts. Some meaningful parts may be phrases—"Once upon a time" or "Thank you." (Preschoolers tend to think of each of these as one unit, not as being composed of four or two words, respectively.) Other units for a young child may be individual words—*Mom, glass, juice.* But in order to "crack the code" in reading an alphabetic language like English or Spanish, children must also begin to perceive smaller units of speech. They need to be able to break words down into syllables and, ultimately, phonemes (individual sounds).

Over the past fifteen years or so, a large and convincing body of research has been amassed, showing that, from first grade on up through elementary school, phonemic awareness is a very strong predictor of reading achievement (Juel, 1991). In essence, what this means is that children who have not developed phonemic awareness by the time they are in first grade are much more likely to be the children who have reading problems in the upper elementary school. Conversely, children who have developed phonemic awareness by this time are much more likely to do all right in reading.

I do not think librarians should be in the business of teaching children decoding skills, i.e., phonics. But it is clear that the beginnings of decoding start long before children go to school. These beginnings lie in rhyming and language play. Initially, phonemic awareness is strictly an oral language skill. Children begin to pay attention to the parts of the words they hear. Note that in order to rhyme, the child has to separate a word, retaining the "ending part" and putting on a new beginning. This breaking down of words into parts is an important principle that becomes more refined and sophisticated as children become capable of perceiving and manipulating smaller and smaller parts. (Eventually a child's knowledge of word parts becomes intertwined with the child's developing knowledge of letters and reading and writing.) But the basic idea is established in early childhood as children engage in word play and rhyming.

Word play and rhyming clearly are the province of librarians, and I encourage you to make poetry and songs an integral part of your library story times and of any other outreach programs with young children. All forms, from nursery rhymes to finger plays to jump rope rhymes to rap songs, are important experiences for young children. And don't forget about songs and rhymes in Spanish (e.g., *Arroz con Leche* by Lulu Delacre [1989]) and other languages for children whose native language is something other than English. In addition, books that play with language are very important to include because they encourage children to reflect on and manipulate the sounds of the language they hear. Think, for instance, of *Sheep in a Jeep* (Shaw, 1986) or *17 Kings and 42 Elephants* (Mahy, 1987) in which children can delight in playing with the sounds they hear in the books.

Language play sounds like a fun thing for young children, and it is. Happily, important cognitive work also gets done in the process of playing with the sounds of language. We often think of learning phonics as dreary drill and practice. It is important for librarians to see the roots of decoding and realize that literature, poetry, and song can play a very key role in its foundations in early childhood.

Literacy and Play

I believe it is helpful to think of two general ways in which literacy and play can come together. The first is already well known to most librarians and is discussed eloquently and powerfully by Vivian Paley: the dramatization of stories. Children can dramatize their own stories and the stories of other authors. Paley's work (1981, 1984, 1990) and studies by McNamee and her colleagues (McNamee, 1987; Harris-Schmidt & McNamee, 1986) convincingly demonstrate the power of children's dramatizing their own stories. Also, Pellegrini and Galda (1993) reviewed ten years of research on symbolic play, much of which was children's reenacting stories they had been told or read. They concluded that such experiences were "important for reading related aspects of early literacy" (p. 172) and even related to significant skill development in early writing. Thus, young children seem to benefit from opportunities to reenact all different kinds of stories.

The second way in which literacy and play can come together relates to the point made at the beginning of this chapter about literacy being a purposeful, functional human activity, not merely an abstract skill that people learn. An important principle for early childhood emergent literacy education is that we try to have literacy function in the lives of young children analogously to the ways it functions in our lives as adults. Adults use written language in the course of daily living routines (paying bills, reading signs, filling out forms, and so forth), entertainment, work, interpersonal communication, as a means of maintaining social relations in their "information networks," and more (Teale, 1986). A general principle that good early childhood educators work by is getting children involved in a wide variety of play activities that have literacy integrally incorporated into them. Whether children are making believe they are grocery shopping, eating in a restaurant, taking a trip on an airplane, being veterinarians, or working at the office, written language can become an integral part of the play. Neuman and Roskos (1990) have written about how to establish early childhood classroom play environments that incorporate authentic literacy props such as food coupons; a telephone book; a calendar; an appointment book; menus; paper for grocery lists; pens, pencils, and other writing instruments; home-made business cards; and sticky notes. Children will use all of these things and many more to make their play come alive and, in the process, will come to understand the functions and power of literacy very directly.

This discussion of children's play and written language presents a good opportunity to point out that, up to now, most of what we have talked about regarding the promotion of preschool children's literacy abilities has involved reading and books. Note how important writing also becomes as we examine this topic. We may tend to associate libraries with books and reading when it comes to young children, but libraries can also be important places for writing. Just as an early childhood teacher provides for different dramatic play centers in the classroom, so could librarians explore the idea of establishing a dramatic play area in the library. The theme and the contents of the area could change from time to time, but the intent would always be the same: to provide an opportunity for children to use written language—reading and writing—as integral parts of their everyday activities of life.

Conclusion

Literacy is a central part of children's readiness for school. An emergent literacy perspective on young children's experiences with written language opens up exciting possibilities for librarians, teachers, and parents alike to promote children's development of reading and writing concepts and strategies. I have tried to outline the general principles of taking an emergent literacy perspective on children's development and to provide some specific suggestions for ways that libraries and librarians can do even more to promote young children's literacy learning. I hasten to point out that these principles and practices apply to all the young children we find ourselves working with, no matter what their language background or their ethnic or cultural heritage.

The key to getting young children off to the right start in reading and writing lies in helping children see literacy as an enjoyable and valued part of their lives. We help them see this not by devising literacy lessons but by creating contexts in which children experience the power and the joys of reading and writing. This process needs to begin as early as possible in children's lives. When children live with literacy, they come to school more than ready; they come as readers and writers ready to learn to read and write conventionally. Libraries and librarians have an important role to play in that process.

Works Cited

Bruner, J. S. (1990). *Acts of meaning.* Cambridge, MA: Harvard University Press.

Chall, J. S., Jacobs, V. A., & Baldwin, L. E. (1990). *The reading crisis: Why poor children fall behind.* Cambridge, MA: Harvard University Press.

Cooperative Children's Book Center, M. V. Lindgren. (Ed.). (1991). *The multicolored mirror: Cultural substance in literature for children and young adults.* Fort Atkinson, WI: Highsmith Press.

Dickinson, D. K., Hao, Z., & He, W. (1993, November). *Book reading: It makes a difference how you do it!* Paper presented at the 83rd Annual Convention of the National Council of the Teachers of English, Pittsburgh, PA.

Dickinson, D. K., & Smith, M. W. (1994). Long-term effects of preschool teachers' book readings on low-income children's vocabulary and story comprehension. *Reading Research Quarterly, 29,* 104–123.

Goldsmith, E. (1993). Translations and transformations: From training to implementation. *Literacy Harvest: The Journal of the Literacy Assistance Center, 2,* (2), 9–16.

Goldsmith, E., & Handel, R. D. (1990). *Family reading: An intergenerational approach to literacy.* Syracuse, NY: New Readers Press.

Greene, E. (1991). *Books, babies, and libraries: Serving infants, toddlers, their parents and caregivers.* Chicago, IL: American Library Association.

Hardy, B. (1977). An approach through narrative. In M. Silka (Ed.), *Towards a poetics of fiction.* Bloomington, IN: Indiana University Press.

Harris, V. J. (Ed.). (1992). *Teaching multicultural literature in grades K-8.* Norwood, MA: Christopher-Gordon.

Harris-Schmidt, G., & McNamee, G. D. (1986). Children as authors and actors: Literacy development through 'basic activities.' *Child Language Teaching and Therapy, 2,* 63–73.

Heath, S. B. (1982). What no bedtime story means: Narrative skills at home and school. *Language in Society, 11,* 49–76.

Juel, C. (1991). Beginning reading. In R. Barr, M. L. Kamil, P. B. Mosenthal, & P. D. Pearson (Eds.), *Handbook of reading research* (Volume II) (pp. 759–788). White Plains, NY: Longman.

Lytle, M. (1994). Just a little bus on wheels but preschoolers get a head start. *American Libraries, 25,* 264–265.

Mandler, J. M., & Johnson, N. S. (1977). Remembrance of things parsed: Story structure and recall. *Cognitive Psychology, 9,* 111–151.

Martinez, M., & Teale, W. H. (1988). Reading in a kindergarten classroom library. *The Reading Teacher, 41,* 568–573.

McNamee, G. D. (1987). The social origins of narrative skills. In M. Hickmann (Ed.), *Social and functional approaches to language and thought* (pp. 287–304). New York: Academic Press.

Miller-Lachmann, L. (1992). *Our family, our friends, our world.* New Providence, NJ: Bowker.

Monsour, M., & Talan, C. (1993). *Library-based family literacy projects.* Chicago, IL: American Library Association.

Neuman, S., & Roskos, K. (1990). Play, print, and purpose: Enriching play environments for literacy development. *The Reading Teacher, 44,* 214–221.

Ninio, A. (1980). Picture-book reading in mother-infant dyads belonging to two subgroups in Israel. *Child Development, 51,* 587–590.

Paley, V. G. (1981). *Wally's stories.* Cambridge, MA: Harvard University Press.

Paley, V. G. (1984). *Boys and girls: Superheroes in the doll corner.* Cambridge, MA: Harvard University Press.

Paley, V. G. (1990). *The boy who would be a helicopter.* Cambridge, MA: Harvard University Press.

Pellegrini, A., & Galda, L. (1993). Ten years after: A reexamination of symbolic play and literacy research. *Reading Research Quarterly, 28,* 163–175

Quezada, S., & Nickse, R. S. (1993). *Community collaborations for family literacy handbook.* New York: Neal-Schuman.

Rochman, H. (1993). *Against borders: Promoting books for a multicultural world.* Chicago: American Library Association.

Rome, L. (1989). Outreach for preschoolers: Project LEAP. *Wilson Library Bulletin, 46,* 39–41.

Segel, E., & Friedberg, J. B. (1991). "Is today liberry day?": Community support for family literacy. *Language Arts, 69,* 654–657.

Snow, C., & Ninio, A. (1986). The contracts of literacy: What children learn from learning to read books. In W. H. Teale & E. Sulzby (Eds.), *Emergent literacy: Writing and reading* (pp. 116–138). Norwood, NJ: Ablex.

Sulzby, E. (1985). Children's emergent reading of favorite storybooks: A developmental study. *Reading Research Quarterly, 20,* 458–481.

Sulzby, E., & Teale, W. (1987). *Young children's storybook reading: Longitudinal study of parent-child interaction and children's independent functioning.* Final report to The Spencer Foundation. Ann Arbor, MI: The University of Michigan.

Sulzby, E., & Teale, W. (1991). Emergent literacy. In R. Barr, M. L. Kamil, P. B. Mosenthal, & P. D. Pearson (Eds.), *Handbook of reading research* (Volume II) (pp. 747–757). White Plains, NY: Longman.

Teale, W. H. (1986). Home background and young children's literacy development. In W. H. Teale & E. Sulzby (Eds.), *Emergent literacy: Writing and reading* (pp. 173–206). Norwood, NJ: Ablex.

Teale, W. H., & Martinez, M. (submitted for publication). The relation between teacher storybook reading style and kindergartners' story comprehension.

Teale, W. H., Martinez, M. G., & McKeown, T. (1994). [Kindergarten children's reading choices and behaviors in three classroom libraries]. Unpublished raw data.

Teale, W. H. & Sulzby, E. (Eds.). (1986). *Emergent literacy: Writing and reading.* Norwood, NJ: Ablex.

Teale, W. H., & Sulzby, E. (1987). Literacy acquisition in early childhood: The roles of access and mediation in storybook reading. In D.A. Wagner (Ed.), *The future of literacy in a changing world* (pp. 111–130). New York: Pergamon.

Teale, W. H., & Sulzby, E. (1989). Emergent literacy: New perspectives on young children's reading and writing development. In D. Strickland & L. Morrow (Eds.), *Emerging literacy: Young children learn to read and write* (pp. 1–15). Newark, DE: International Reading Association.

Yokota, J. (1993). Issues in selecting multicultural children's literature. *Language Arts, 70,* 156–167.

Children's Books Cited

Delacre, L. (1989). *Arroz con leche.* New York: Scholastic.

Ginsburg, M. (1972). *The chick and the duckling.* Illustrated by J. Aruego & A. Dewey. New York: Macmillan.

Machotka, H. (1992). *Breathtaking noses.* New York: Morrow Junior Books.

Mahy, M. (1987). *17 kings and 42 elephants.* Illustrated by P. MacCarthy. New York: Dial Books.

Martin, B. (1967). *Brown bear, brown bear, What do you see?* Illustrated by E. Carle. New York: Holt, Rinehart & Winston.

Morris, A. (1989). *Bread, bread, bread.* Photographs by K. Heyman. New York: Mulberry Books.

Shaw, N. (1986). *Sheep in a jeep.* Illustrated by M. Apple. Boston: Houghton Mifflin.

Tarrant, G. (1983). *Frogs.* Illustrated by D. Maxwell. New York: G.P. Putnam's Sons.

Wood, A. (1984). *The napping house.* Illustrated by D. Wood. San Diego: Harcourt Brace Jovanovich.

Yabuuchi, M. (1981). *Whose baby?* New York: Philomel.

CHAPTER 7

Developing
the Prototype

Prototype: 1. An original type, form, or instance that serves as a model on which later stages are based or judged. **2.** An early and typical example.

(American Heritage Dictionary)

The intent of the prototype is to envision the future of public library service to young children in light of the first of the national education goals. The ideas illuminated in the previous chapters of this volume informed and enlivened the discussions and debates that took place during prototype development. Consequently, while the new vision documented in the prototype respects the tradition of public library service to young children, it also acknowledges the need to expand that tradition to include emerging theories within the academic disciplines of early childhood education and child development.

The actual work involved in producing the prototype took place in small-group sessions. Throughout the Achieving School Readiness Institute, participants met in discussion groups to consider the speaker presentations. These discussions were centered on two questions:

1. What was the speaker telling us?
2. How can the knowledge gained from the presentation enhance library service to young children?

The combined knowledge of the Institute participants, their varied backgrounds and experiences, as well as presentations on exemplary library programs for young children, all added depth and richness to the discussion of these questions and the development of the prototype.

Subsequent discussion was guided by a more specific set of questions intended to facilitate prototype development:

1. What services should public libraries emphasize by the year 2000 to help children enter school ready to learn?
2. What skills will parents, early childhood educators, child care providers, and librarians need to implement such services?
3. What new organizational structures will be needed to implement these services?
4. What resources will be needed to implement these services?
5. What are the next steps?

The final discussions that led to the development of the prototype were also influenced by three supplementary documents:

1. The National Association for the Education of Young Children (NAEYC) *Position Statement on School Readiness* (1990)
2. The Association for Library Service to Children (ALSC) *Competencies for Librarians Serving Children in Public Libraries* (1989)
3. *Planning and Role Setting for Public Libraries: A Manual of Options and Procedures* (1987).

The NAEYC *Position Statement* is based on the premise that any discussion of school readiness must begin with an awareness of at least three critical factors:

1. the diversity and inequity of children's early life experiences;
2. the wide range of variation in young children's develop-
    ment and learning; and
3. the degree to which school expectations of children enter-
    ing kindergarten are reasonable, appropriate, and suppor-
    tive of individual differences (NAEYC, 1990, p. 21).

Guided by the statement of the NAEYC, prototype developers were ever mindful of the "basic principle of child development that there is tremendous normal variability both
among children of the same chronological age and within an
individual child" (NAEYC, 1990, p. 21).

During prototype development, similar attention was
given to the ALSC *Competencies* that are grounded on the
premise that "the philosophical basis for children's services in
public libraries is full access for children to library materials
and services" (ALSC, 1989). The ALSC *Competencies* include
sixty-two specific items arranged in seven broad categories.

1. Knowledge of client group
2. Administrative and management skills
3. Communication skills
4. Materials and collection development
5. Programming skills
6. Advocacy, public relations, and networking skills
7. Professionalism and professional development

Planning and Role Setting for Public Libraries (1987)
defines and describes a menu of eight roles for public libraries. In following the guidelines set forth in this planning manual, libraries are encouraged to select appropriate roles for
themselves in light of community priorities and the institu-
tional mission statements. Of chief concern to the developers
of the prototype was the role of "Preschoolers' Door to Learning." Libraries selecting this role accept as a primary responsibility the task of encouraging "young children to develop an
interest in reading and learning through services for children,
and for parents and children together" (*Planning and Role
Setting*, 1987, p. 28). In regard to the achievement of the first
of the national education goals, prototype developers consid-

ered this the most important role public libraries should seek to fulfill.

Throughout the prototype document, much attention is given to cooperation and collaboration between librarians and members of the early care and education community. In regard to young children, care and education take place continuously and simultaneously. When librarians work with toddlers and preschoolers, they join with parents, teachers, child care workers, health care providers, and a host of other individuals who are concerned with the care and education of young children. The prototype encourages children's librarians to become more actively involved with members of the early care and education community, and as a consequence, to become more knowledgeable and empathetic toward members of that community. While librarians have much to offer, they also have much to learn. A cooperative-collaborative relationship between librarians and early care and education providers will benefit not only these two groups, but also the children both seek to serve.

The prototype also emphasizes the nurturing of young children and their families. While library materials remain an important item for consideration, the emphasis of the prototype is on the developing child, with library materials seen as a means for such development. Opportunities for play in a print-rich, story-filled environment are imperative to achievement of the school readiness goal. Libraries must make a fundamental shift in their philosophies and their facilities if such opportunities are to be provided.

An emphasis on the child and on nurturing is underscored by an awareness and appreciation for developmentally appropriate practice. Bredekamp & Rosegrant (1992) define this as "practices that better reflect what is known about how children develop and learn (what is age appropriate) and practices that are more sensitive to individual and cultural variation (what is individually appropriate)" (p. 3). Incorporation of the precepts of developmentally appropriate practice into library programs and services allows librarians to consider more fully the educational implications of their work. At the same time, these practices free librarians from the burden of traditional teaching conventions. There is no predetermined set of skills librarians must help preschoolers develop. The intent instead, is to predispose young children to the joys of learning.

The prototype, which follows, is presented as a separate, standalone document. It is intended for use by a wide cross section of library practitioners, administrators, and supporters. The future envisioned in the prototype is only beginning. The work of specific libraries, library support groups, and individual librarians is needed to make the vision a reality.

Works Cited

Association for Library Service to Children. (1989). *Competencies for librarians serving children.* Chicago, IL: American Library Association.

Bredekamp, S. & Rosegrant, T. (Eds.). (1992). *Reaching potentials: Appropriate curriculum and assessment for young children,* vol. 1. Washington, DC: National Association for the Education of Young Children.

National Association for the Education of Young Children. (1990). NAEYC position statement on school readiness. *Young Children, 46* (1), 21–23.

Planning and role setting for public libraries: A manual of options and procedures. (1987). Chicago, IL: American Library Association.

Prototype of Library Service to Young Children and Their Families

By the year 2000, all children will enter school ready to learn.

The First of the National Education Goals

Prologue

The National Education Goals were initiated by the nation's Governors and the President in 1989 and enacted into Public Law 103–227, the "Goals 2000: Educate America Act," in March of 1994. In May of 1994, the Graduate School of Library and Information Science at the University of Texas at Austin hosted a five-day Institute funded by the U.S. Department of Education titled "Achieving School Readiness: Public Libraries and the First of the National Education Goals." The purpose of the Institute was threefold:

- to broaden understanding of the critical dimensions of school readiness

- to examine the services provided to preschool children in public libraries in light of that understanding

- to develop a prototype of library service to preschool children to assist in the achievement of the school readiness goal.

139

The prototype is the work of a national group of administrators and practitioners of early childhood education programs, state library youth consultants, university faculty members from colleges of education, psychology, child development, and schools of library and information science, children's services coordinators from regional library systems, and children's library practitioners. Documents used for authoritative background material during prototype development included:

- The National Association for the Education of Young Children (NAEYC) *Position Statement on School Readiness*

- The Association for Library Service to Children (ALSC) *Competencies for Librarians Serving Children in Public Libraries*

- *Planning and Role Setting for Public Libraries: A Manual of Options and Procedures.*

The prototype focuses on the services, skills, attitudes, resources, and organizational structures needed to provide quality library service to young children, their families, and caregivers. The purpose of the prototype is to assist public libraries in being active and effective partners in ensuring that all children have the opportunity to succeed in school and become lifelong learners.

The Prototype

An essential mission of public libraries is to ensure that young children receive services and support that help to prepare them for success in school and to become lifelong learners. This mission is accomplished by:

- adopting the role of "Preschoolers' Door to Learning" as a national priority in public libraries

- centering children's services around the developmental needs of children and their families

- building coalitions and developing a shared vision with the early care and education community.

Adoption of this mission for public libraries affects the services libraries provide, calls for specific skills and attitudes, requires new organizational structures, and demands sufficient resources.

Services

Library services for young children and their families must be responsive to the whole child, his or her family, and caregivers. Services must address the child prenatally through age eight. Services must be developed in consultation and collaboration with the early care and education community.

Service priorities include:

- Participatory programs designed for children's developmental levels rather than an age-specific audience
- Family-based participatory programs that highlight cultural diversity and appeal to multigenerational audiences
- Informational and educational programs, developed in partnership with the early care and education community, for parents and child care providers that enhance understanding of child development, early learning, emergent literacy, prenatal services, child health care issues, community support services, and library resources
- Informational and educational programs for library administrators and trustees that heighten awareness and commitment to services for young children and their families
- Outreach programs that extend the audience for library services to the larger community, particularly those who are not currently library customers
- Family literacy projects designed to increase both the quantity and quality of print-related interactions between parents and their children
- Information and referral services designed to link children and their families to community support services

- Consulting services for children, parents, and the early care and education community, including all personnel, licensed and unlicensed care providers, privately and publicly funded organizations.

Attitudes and Skills

Library staff must embrace the belief that all children and their families are library customers of primary importance and that librarians share responsibility for ensuring that children succeed in school and become lifelong learners. Librarians must form partnerships with parents, early care and education providers, and other community-based agencies serving youth to provide appropriate services and support for young children and their families.

This belief is supported and demonstrated through:

- Respect for and value of children and their families

- Enthusiasm for learning new skills and acquiring new knowledge related to child development, early learning, emergent literacy, multiculturalism, and linguistic diversity

- Commitment to the library as a living, breathing organism that welcomes human interaction and responds to human needs both inside and outside the library building

- Establishment of an atmosphere that welcomes change and encourages flexibility in the provision of services commensurate with levels of customer diversity and need

- Commitment to partnerships based on mutual respect with early care and education providers as well as other youth- and family-serving agencies

- Active participation as advocates for young children and their families in political and social arenas at local, state, and national levels.

To serve young children, their parents, and caregivers effectively, librarians' repertoire of skills, as well as their knowledge base, must be increased and enhanced.

Requisite skills and knowledge include:

- Knowledge and understanding of child development and how children learn
- Written and oral communication skills
- Public speaking skills
- Knowledge and use of new and developing information technologies
- Knowledge of evaluation and assessment techniques in order to collect and interpret data regarding the effectiveness of library services in relation to the developmental levels of children
- Creative thinking and problem-solving skills
- Skills in negotiation and conflict resolution
- Enhanced skills for library programming, including storytelling and the development of personal narratives
- Awareness of and ability to apply marketing and public relations techniques
- Utilization of networking skills to forge partnerships and build coalitions with other professionals and agencies serving children and their families
- Political skills and acumen in order to effectively serve as child and family advocates.

Organizational Structures

Realizing the vision of service and support for young children and their families will require new organizational structures within individual libraries as well as in the broader library community. Changes will be required in library policies, in personnel deployment, in facilities design and utilization, in patterns of communication, and in education for librarianship.

Policies required:

- Revision of library mission statements in order to place child and family services as the top priority

- Acceptance of "Preschoolers' Door to Learning" as a primary role for public libraries across the nation
- Adoption of library policies and procedures that respect all library customers, regardless of age and ability level.

Personnel needs and roles include:

- A children's librarian on every library staff, a children's advocate on every library board, a children's coordinator in every library system and network, and a children's consultant in all state library agencies
- Children's librarians included at the policy making level, serving as equal partners on library administrative and management teams
- Children's librarians authorized to create partnerships and participate in coalitions, and encouraged to establish community boards for child and family advocacy
- Library staff and volunteers trained and utilized to enhance service to multilingual and culturally diverse customers and to children with special needs.

Facilities requirements:

- Adequate space allocated for children's collections, programs, and activities
- Child-centered environments that are well designed, accessible, and developmentally appropriate
- Space designed for families and for learning and readiness activity centers.

Communication needs:

- Establish mechanisms for communication among librarians, the early care and education community, state libraries, regional education centers, and professional organizations.

Professional education changes:

- Integrate early childhood education practice into youth services course work in schools of library and information science

- Integrate children's services issues into required library and information science course work

- Develop continuing education programs that emphasize early childhood education theory and practice and explore children's services issues

- Develop partnerships with master practitioners for productive practicums, internships, and field work experiences for aspiring youth services librarians

- Encourage early childhood education departments to include information regarding library services and resources in their course offerings

- Develop a research agenda in response to the needs of library practitioners and disseminate research results

- Develop collaborative research projects with practitioners and academic colleagues from other disciplines

- Develop sources of funding for research

- Work to ensure retention of children's specialists as tenured faculty in schools of library and information science

- Recruit doctoral students with an interest in children's and family services in public libraries.

Resources

Library resources are the basis for the delivery of service and must be equitably distributed to ensure the attainment of the library's mission. In order to serve and support young children and their families, funding must be secured through public and private sources. Grant funding for youth services projects must be pursued. Governmental support must be sought through the establishment of a LSCA Title dedicated to early childhood and through specified funding in every child care or related bill presented to state legislatures or the U.S. Congress with libraries named as recipients.

Funding must be allocated for:

- Up-to-date materials in a wide variety of formats to accommodate diversity in developmental levels and abilities, cultural and language heritages, learning-style preferences, and family traditions

- Manipulative materials that are developmentally appropriate for use in learning and readiness centers

- Professional materials for parents, librarians, and the early care and education community

- Vans and other vehicles to facilitate outreach services

- Qualified staff to design and deliver developmentally appropriate services to children and their families through partnerships with the early care and education community.

A Call to Action

VIRGINIA H. MATHEWS

I will begin by stating five basic beliefs upon which this call to action is based.

> I believe that librarians and library resources/programs may be and can be recognized as an essential part of real change and the solutions to many social and economic problems. I also believe that libraries are for everyone and not, as many people seem still to contend, bastions of the middle class.

> I believe that literacy—even or especially in an age saturated with technology—is of paramount importance in making the difference between self-realization and failure. The comments of a highly placed White House aide, quoted in *Newsweek* within the past year are enlightening: "You campaign and win on TV, but you govern in print. Ultimately, people think (with words) through print—that's the way

VIRGINIA H. MATHEWS is Consultant for Family Literacy Projects for the Center for the Book in the Library of Congress and Coordinator since 1992 for its Library-Museum Head Start Partnership project funded by the Head Start Bureau of the U.S. Department of Health and Human Services. In addition, she serves as an advisor to NCLIS on youth issues and works as an editor for Neal-Schuman Publishing. She was the lead writer of the "Omnibus Children and Youth Literacy Initiative" that was adopted as the first priority of the 1991 White House Conference on Library and Information Services. A "lover of history," she is the proud daughter of a historian, an American Indian member of the Osage tribe who wrote a number of books.

issues get framed" (Alter, 1993, p. 37). I do not believe for a moment that the time for printed words and thoughts has passed. Literacy is an essential base for earned self-esteem.

I believe that children's librarians along with their colleagues in the early care and education community are ready to assume transformational leadership rather than transactional leadership roles. Transactional leaders react to issues and opportunities, to day-to-day events, and may have little taste for risk taking. Transformational leaders, on the other hand, take initiatives that make things happen, creating new solutions and approaches as they go. They are those who take, with Robert Frost, "the road less traveled by." They enjoy inventing their own jobs and (their own) futures and they expect positive results and changes as the result of their actions. Such leadership is never really comfortable because it is always creating new possibilities and problems to be solved, often at the cost of leisure and personal well-being.

I believe in new productive ways of working. The old ways are marred too often by competition and conflict; the new are marked by cooperation, coalition building, contact, and cultural exchanges. Archibald MacLeish, poet and fighter for freedom of the mind, envisioned librarians empowered for leadership when, as Librarian of Congress (1939–44) he said, "Libraries must be active, not passive agents of the democratic process. Libraries are the only institutions in the U.S. capable of dealing with the contemporary crisis in American life in terms and under conditions which give promise of success. Libraries owe an affirmative obligation to the people. The people have a right to such service" (Mathews, 1975, p. 47). Fifty years later people are demanding to be plugged in to the power source for information, inspiration, and empowerment! How up-to-date that sounds!

Finally, I believe that all individuals, not just the elite, can become competent thinkers, reasoners, and problem solvers. Opportunities for such learning must be in the curriculum of all "tracks" in all schools for all children and young people. Lauren Resnick, cognitive psychologist at the University of Pittsburgh, suggests that "this is precisely the challenge ahead of us; to make thinking and problem solving a regular part of the school program for all the population. . . . What this implies is that improving basic skills is not a sufficient objective for the education reform movement or for how we often conceive of literacy programs" (Rockefeller Foundation, 1989, p. 28–29). Higher order thinking skills, which we include in the scope of high literacy skills, can empower low-income single mothers, those with dead-end jobs or no jobs at all, and the young with too limited objectives and self-expectations. Higher order thinking skills permit one to follow a path of action not fully specified in advance. The total path is not visible (mentally speaking) from any single vantage point. Such thinking often yields multiple solutions, each with costs and benefits, rather than a single unique and satisfying solution. It requires the application of multiple criteria which sometimes conflict with one another. Such thinking requires self-regulation of the thinking process without anyone to call the correct plays, and learning to make choices; it involves finding meaning and finding structure in apparent disorder. Real effort is needed—the effort to make linkages, to elaborate, to compare and judge. Learning to do such thinking can and should begin in very early childhood.

The Magic of Early Childhood

What do you remember about being three or four or five? If you have a good recall of yourself in those years, you will not be surprised how very important they are in forming a person. Working with children of these ages as you all do, even seeing how they behave and perceive is not quite the same as feeling it inside. What you recall are probably fragments and flashes, but if you think hard you will probably remember yourself as a person who saw and heard and responded to the world around you. Children of these ages do. They see and absorb what is going on. They especially absorb behavior that is modeled for them.

My mother modeled creativity, high expectations, curiosity, and laughter. As musical and theatrical events critic for a Los Angeles paper, she often took me with her to sit in the second seat critics are given. By virtue of a long afternoon nap and being wakened shortly before curtain time, I heard William Beebe lecture, standing beside his bathysphere, on his pioneering adventures under the ocean. I also was taken to see many, many dancers. One artist that made a very great impression was Harry Lauder. He was a musical comedy star from Scotland. He always wore a kilt and played the bagpipes. Some of his lyrics were downright risqué, but very delightful. They passed right over my head, of course. I thought when he said "roamin' in the gloamin' with my bonnie by my side" they were probably looking at the sunset, but they weren't. But it was okay.

Short poems were always posted on the icebox (that cold food storage place in the kitchen that I still find hard to call a refrigerator). Back at age two, the large linenette book of *Peter Rabbit* was so familiar that, as the pages were turned, I knew exactly where Peter sneezed and was discovered by Mr. McGregor, and I sneezed with him. I often went with Mother at four or five when she gave her dance recitals at places like the Azusa Women's Club and grew quite accustomed to hearing her called by her professional name. Such experiences fostered social competence (I had to meet people and be gracious and talk with them) and laid the base for the reading I had already begun to enjoy. It was at three and four, too, that my father and I lay on our backs in the garden under a tree while he showed me how to use binoculars and identify the birds. I did not go to school until I entered fourth grade when I was eight. I had a good deal of private instruction, some in things perhaps that most first, second, and third graders do not get. We had crafts. We had clay, which Mother modeled with me. I learned a couple of languages, most of which I have forgotten now. I learned a lot about music, a lot about art. I learned a lot of things about people. So when the good sisters at St. Mary's in Peekskill said, "Well, she is a little young for fourth grade," Mother said, "Oh, she will fit in beautifully." And since that was the expectation, I did. What else could I do?

Challenges of Parenting Today

My purpose in sharing these personal memories, and perhaps stirring for you some of your own, is to compare them sharply with the early influences and experiences that perhaps a majority of two to five year olds are undergoing now. Many families are beset and despairing and unable to provide a base of stimulation and interests that prepare the way for language and literacy for their ready-to-learn children. If parents cannot or will not ensure that their children's minds develop to the fullest, someone else must. Our whole future is at stake. Because, as the wonderful saying of the traditionally black colleges goes, "A mind is a terrible thing to waste."

Use them or lose them. The lessons learned by neuroscientists about the results of deprivation, leading to permanent stunting of brains and the ability to learn, surfaced recently in a report of the Carnegie Corporation about the plight of American children at risk. These lessons have been responsible in no small part for the new attention being given to the birth to three years age group, including some provisions in the recent reauthorization that lower the age at which Head Start programs become available.

Reaching Out:
To Partners, to Parents, to Youth

Does this mean that children's librarians must become psychologists, child development experts, nutritionists, social workers, and health care providers? No—but it does mean that librarians who work with very young children, helping them to get ready for learning and for life, must work in a team relationship with and build coalitions with professionals, paraprofessionals, and volunteers from these and other areas. Readiness as we all realize is a very slippery term. Children are ready as soon as they are born to live, and living is learning. The youngest children librarians are likely to see much of are the sum total of what they have already observed, felt, touched, and had modeled for them—their environment, the interactions with siblings, and above all with parents and other caregivers. The nuances and tones of speech, the atmosphere of safety or insecurity (everything that has happened in the life of the child) have already been internalized and made their mark. The readiness Goal One envisions includes everything that has happened in the life of the child that prepares him or her for the wider world of formal instruction and learning. The success of this learning—how well it "takes" with a particular child—will depend in large part on how well it relates to what the child already knows. If the material that is put before him or her to absorb and ponder is way out of sync with what is brought to that learning, we have a problem. Areas of learning the child brings include emotional-social, aesthetic-creative, linguistic, physical, moral-spiritual, and more. Rachel Carson, who was one of the first to clue us in on the destruction of the environment also tells us: "If a child is to keep alive the inborn sense of wonder . . . he needs the companionship of at least one adult who can share it, rediscovering with him the joy, excitement, and mystery of the world we live in" (Carson, 1956). The operative words here, I believe are "share" and "joy," but it is hard or impossible to share a sense of joy if you have never felt it. We must help all we work with—especially parents—to realize that learning flourishes when enjoyment enters into it, and that books and reading can be a shared and social activity, not only a solitary one.

A group of pediatricians practicing in different parts of the country have for the past few years been prescribing books to be shared by children and parents who come to their clinics. This is happening in the Boston area, in Cleveland, in upper New York state, and in other places as well. They are publishing a great deal in the pediatric journals and reporting an amazing fact: in studying the results of this effort it has been found that this shared activity, this positive interaction with a parent or other significant adult, provides a shield or antidote—in effect it helps to immunize the child—against some of the fears and insecurities of her surroundings, and actually induces better health and facilitates emergent literacy (Neddlman & Zuckerman, 1992).

So many studies have shown three vital bases for literacy development and sustained literacy habits that we no longer have to mention individual studies by name to be believed. They are, of course:

exposure to words, songs, chants, and books from earliest infancy
being read aloud to frequently from a year or so
seeing reading modeled and enjoyed by parents or other significant adults.

The illiteracy of parents and other adults around them deeply affects children's literacy and learning development. The majority of children and young people in juvenile corrections have lived with one parent, often illiterate, and socialize with the children of illiterates. Imagine, if you can, the difference early intervention for all children would make if parents could be fully involved in family literacy projects. Programs could be provided in library buildings, in housing projects, in isolated rural areas, in child care and Head Start centers, in drug rehabilitation centers, and in health clinics for teen mothers. One of the most pathetic and dreadful lacks that I see is in the kind of rehabilitation older kids in corrections or in rehabilitation get—practically nothing at all. They are released "cured," but not cured, because they have not been given anything that keeps them from going out and doing it over again. The situation is tragic. No other professional who touches the lives of children has more or better resources than do librarians to answer the age-old questions, often unspoken: Who am I? Who could I become? Where do I belong? Do I have a future? No other professionals can do a better job of bringing together two or even three generations around concepts and ideas.

Nurturing Vital Alliances

We need to include in our coalitions of youth advocates members of the media, such as newspaper columnists— explaining to them how librarians as part of a team can address the goals they envision (and often write about) for kids and be part of the solutions to social upheaval. We often see these columns in periodicals or the local paper and say, "Oh good. I am glad he is saying that." But how often do we call him up and say "Terrific, I am glad you are writing about it. Let me send you some material. Can I come see you? Let's talk." We must do more of that. I know time is short. It's short for everybody. But time is also short for all of us in terms of the children. The kid who is four years old today, will be fourteen in ten years. And if she is a girl, she well may have a little baby. Will she know enough to parent that baby effectively? Will she know about reading aloud and talking to it, and saying little nonsense rhymes? In a world where everything is crisis, and hard, and stressful, is it fair to ask young women out of the blue to exude and portray joy, to model thoughtfulness and serenity for their infants? These are things we have to think hard about.

Government officials at all levels need to be told that we are effective in providing a sense of self-worth and esteem in children, showing them that there are choices to be made and how to make them. We believe that literacy in its fullest sense provides empowerment, that the insights, expectations, perspectives, attitudes, and skills librarians present to children can make a big difference in their lives.

In my recent experiences in talking with members of Congress and Congressional staff, there are several things I have heard, misconceptions that we have to do something about. There was the congressman who told a staff person that poor people don't use libraries, they don't need them. Another said that librarians don't do anything to train parents! The staff member of the Juvenile Justice and Delinquency Division of the Department of Justice also did not know much of what librarians are about. The "Ounce of Prevention" section of the crime bill authorizes funds to try to help children go straight, to avoid idle "hanging out" and go positively into life, not negatively. Libraries are not mentioned of course, in the entire document. When I called up the man in charge of that office for the Justice Department, I told him that in reading the crime bill, which I had gotten from my Congressman, I had found several suggestions of things libraries are already doing. I asked, why not put the word libraries in there, because if it is not in there nobody is going to know we are doing those things, are expected to do them, or can apply for funds to do them. He said, "That is an interesting idea. Now, just give me a for-instance." "For instance," I said, "it says here that after-school programs need to be developed so children will be doing positive things in a safe environment with some adult supervision, and with help for homework and so forth." I told him that hundreds of libraries across this country are doing exactly this same thing as we spoke (it was 3 o'clock in the afternoon) for thousands and thousands of children. They are getting volunteers from RSVP and other places to come in and help them with their homework and help them with things they need to think about. And he said, "Really? That is very interesting; I did not know that."

We get resentful when people say things like that. But it is our fault. We have not let them know—not sufficiently, not specifically, not aggressively enough. We put out the news that libraries are good places, but not that we are offering "ounces of prevention" every day. We do not keep hammering them. You know the story about getting the donkey to do what you want him to do. You have to hit him with a two-by-four before you talk to him. This, in effect, is what we are saying. This does not go well with our womanly image. But we have to make some changes in ourselves if we are going to behave in this new way. We must never be rude, strident, or shrewish, but must learn to lose our fear of rejection in our passion for getting done what we know is right. When you have won a staff advocate of a member of House or Senate, an individual or committee, prepare him or her to talk to a committee effectively. When someone says, "Libraries don't teach parenting skills," prepare him to say, "Oh yes they do! I have here a list of places where they are having workshops for parents, and working with teenage mothers, and working to try to help people to become better parents, not just laying the groundwork for reading, but also teaching nutrition and places to go to for help." Policy makers do not read library professional periodicals. They read their home-state news and watch news broadcasts, but they are not getting our message. We must find a way to tell them what we are doing that relates to programs they are authorizing and funding.

Teaching the Higher Uses of Information

Gifted Georgia writer Flannery O'Connor wrote: "You have to push as hard as the age that pushes against you." The age that pushes young people pushes them too often into crime and failure and often death, not merely with grinding poverty and lack of material well-being, but also with toxic ideas. It is not something that has happened out of the blue, we—the society—have created it. Much of it comes with trickle-down culture that trumpets the idea that the good life consists of satisfying every (single) impulse we have. Impulse buying is what TV ads live on. They train the kids to say, "Oh, I've got to have Cheerios instead of Corn Flakes because that's what is on television." These ideas were expressed by George Will, an editorial writer I don't usually care for, but who often comes up with some very interesting ideas. While discussing the ideas of Edwin Delattre, Dean of Boston University's School of Education, Will says "When a twelve-year-old boy turns without a word and shoots dead a seven-year-old girl because she "diss'ed" him by standing on his shadow, he is pushed by the age. He possesses a prickly sensitivity about his self-esteem and is incapable of distinguishing an action from a motive" (Will, 1993, p. 84). Delattre believes that we are losing "the struggle between philosophy and power, between reason and passion. . . . The age has obliterated human magnificence . . . with the observation that everyone has flaws, therefore no one merits emulation." Since the idea has taken hold that "there is no moral heritage worth 'imposing' on children . . . their selection of values may be regarded as a matter of taste." Delattre thinks that this is why so many students (at the college level, at the high school level) never criticize a proposition by saying "'I believe you are mistaken for the following reasons.'. . . Instead they give autobiographical reports such as 'I'm not comfortable with that.' Students regard such reports about their feelings as final and no more in need of justification than the assertion 'I don't like brussel sprouts'" (Will, 1993, p. 84).

We must help children—from earliest childhood—to learn to "push against the age" with information literacy, critical literacy, cultural literacy, so that they will understand that not all decisions in life "are motivated by the desire to acquire power for advantage over others," and that many can only be made satisfactorily when based on information rather than feelings. We must show them that choices and worlds exist other than the ones which seem to trap them. Perhaps above all we must introduce them to the concept of love that transcends biology and egoism and the urge toward the conquest of mere sexuality. Where better than libraries to find the images of sacrifice and sharing that provide keys to nourishment for the emotionally starved. Emotional starvation, not sexual hunger, drives a good portion of the more than a million young girls who have illegitimate babies each year so "I can have someone of my own to love me." And it's not just poor girls, or girls at risk, it's middle-class, upper-class, all kinds of girls, to whom a child is important because it will be someone that has to love them, at least as long as it depends upon them.

This kind of emotional hunger is something that we have to remember to feed and nourish. We can do it. We have the materials to do it. We have tales of romance and selflessness, doing things for the greater good, doing things for other people. These are concepts that some of these children do not know exist, since they have never seen them in action.

Politics of Youth Services

Politics are becoming more and more the business of all advocates for children, including of course children's librarians. The White House Conference on Libraries and Information Services was held in 1991. We worked very hard for more than five years before that conference to make sure that going into it, and hopefully coming out of it, there would be some real, serious, important, significant attention to children's and youth services in libraries. I think all of us who worked on that believed that we could do it, that it could happen, and it did. We contacted a number of organizations that are child and youth oriented, the Child Welfare League of America, the Children's Defense Fund, the National Black Child Development Institute, the American Association of Retired Persons, the Parent-Teacher Association, and many other organizations. We told them what we were going to do and enlisted their help. Twelve of these groups gave us statements of approval and endorsement of "Kids Need Libraries," the base policy paper we prepared two years in advance.

We took those comments, and the youth resolutions from all the state conferences that took place in the years before the conference, and we sent those to every single conference delegate in advance. We also sent something we called a "Compact with Youth." We planned a strategy for the conference. We did what they do in Congress—we tried to figure out who were the people we knew were going to stand by us, who were the people who were on the fence and needed to be worked with. We did a real political job—nothing wrong with a political job; it worked perfectly. When we got to the conference, we knew where every single one of the delegates was going to be in small-group discussions. We made sure that somehow, the people who had been assigned to those small groups were briefed, so that they would speak up.

We used what came to be called during the conference "the purple paper." It was the portion of "Kids Need Libraries" that said what the federal responsibility should be—what would be needed. The first portion of it, which dealt with school libraries, has gone directly into the Elementary and Secondary Education Act (ESEA), which is the school library amendment. It passed the House by a very large margin. It has also passed the Senate. When the bill finally comes through with funding once again earmarked for school library resources, it will be a triumph for all youth services and a tribute to the power of the White House Conference process.

The 1991 White House Conference was set up with about 1,000 participants, but only one-half of them could be librarians or in library-related positions, such as library trustees or Friends of Libraries. The others had to be government officials or citizens who were not librarians. Therefore only one-quarter of the delegates were librarians. And I'll tell you honestly, that if it had been decided only by the librarians at that conference, the Omnibus Youth Initiative would not have been the first priority. Never. No way. It was a priority by a huge margin of a straw vote that was taken the evening before the voting, to see what the states thought was the priority. And we won, because of the concern for youth from the lay people, especially the government officials. I talked to a juvenile court judge from Arkansas who said, in response to my lobbying, "Of course I will vote for it. If all of the kids that come before me in juvenile court had used libraries and learned to read they wouldn't be there." People, real honest-to-God people, a lot of them, know this. People who have had contact with kids, and social, economic, and educational problems.

So, we won that one. However, the response was rather cold from many of the powerhouses in library-land. "How come? Youth services isn't any more important than networks for goodness sakes. Why aren't networks first? Or marketing? Or something else?" Well, that's the way it was. We worked for it and we got it. And now we are working like the dickens to get it implemented. And that's going to take a long time. But the ESEA Amendment, which implements the first section of our initiative, and also the Head Start reauthorization of 1994 are a part of that implementation. We mentioned Head Start by name in the portion of the bill where we talked about early childhood programs. And that was not accidental.

We do have some very, very firm friends and advocates in the state libraries and in the public libraries. I don't mean to imply that we do not. Even in the academic libraries we have some very good friends, but not as many as we should have. The process for reauthorization of the Library Services and Construction Act is due to begin in 1995. And it looks, as of now, as if children's and youth services are going to get a substantial mandate for a set-aside in that reauthorization. It is the Congress that decides. But at least it is likely that the library world will speak with one voice to the Congress. The public libraries, the state libraries, the urban libraries, all the other people who have a finger in the pie have put all their data in, and youth services have been made a priority area. Why? Because social need has caught up with us, and many of our library colleagues recognize this. Do not forget that. We are in the mainstream now. Social need and economic need have found us. We have been here all the time but they have found us, and found in what we do some solutions to enormous problems.

What does it take to implement a vision as inclusive as that propounded in "Kids Need Libraries" or the Omnibus initiative? You need a policy base. You need to know what needs to be done. How to do it? Where are we (that's statistics) in achieving it? And why does it matter whether it is done or not done? What will happen if nothing good happens through libraries for children and young people? We have to be able to tell that graphically, and with drama—because some terrible things are going to happen to this society if it survives at all. We must build the perception that what happens at the national level deeply influences what happens in each state, the most crowded city, or the smallest hamlet. We are often guilty of very small-scale thinking. People often say, yes, the Washington Office is doing this and that, but that's happening at the federal level and what I have to worry about is what's here at home. That's true in a way, but not true in another way. Because all of these bills, if we successfully get them through Congress, come down to the local level. The bills need to include the mandate that libraries, along with other agencies, are part of the solution to the problem of what happens to kids. And that is going to affect you, for better or for worse.

We have to have a personal vision and passion in expressing it. Compelling convictions, and the ability to communicate this to all-comers without fear of rejection. You have to have the hide of the rhinoceros for this kind of work. If people reject you, it is not because you are pretty or not pretty, or they like you or do not like you. It is because they have their own agenda. And if you are rejected, you bounce right back. You do not get upset about it. You have to try to be without self-consciousness or uncertainty. Uncertainty is a weakness. And people will get you at the point of your uncertainty. In other words, you must be armed with passionate belief, capable of sweeping others along into understanding.

Performance

You are always performing as a child advocate, an advocate for equity in learning, in confidence, in motivation. Wherever. Whenever. You are always performing. Networks operate in mysterious ways. And you never know who is watching and listening, whether at the beauty parlor, the barber shop, a party, or at your own desk. There are always people judging you—for yourself—but also for who you are and what you believe in. You are a child advocate. And you need to exude this all the time.

Persistence

This is really what political action is made from. And remember, political action is action with and by people. We are not talking about anything terribly esoteric. We are talking about actions of and for people. This is perhaps the most important of all. When you want something more than anyone else does not want you to have it, you are going to get it. But only if you never give up. It may take three mailings of the same material to the legislative assistant who never can find it. They ALL cannot find it sometimes, usually Friday afternoon, when it is needed Monday morning. People do not return phone calls. You need to not be bashful. After a decent interval, you call them again. And if they have an answering machine you say, "I think maybe your machine is not working. I called you last Tuesday and we do need to talk. Would you call me?" And you do it again if necessary.

Remember when you are beginning to think that everyone by now must have heard your message, and either accepted it or rejected it, that is the time to redouble your efforts. Because most of them have not.

Purity of Purpose

This is a very important weapon in your arsenal. This sounds like a funny one. But it means you are not afraid to do anything or ask anyone for anything, because you are not getting anything personal from it (okay, you get your job; but you would probably have that anyway). The fact is, if you can convince people that you are not performing with passion and persistence for an ulterior motive, that you are doing it only because service to children and young people is a public good, is a public necessity, you will prevail. And if you really believe that, you can make them believe it.

Things You Can Do Right Now

First, empower parents, families, and caregivers of at-risk preschool children to continue to support that child's learning after he or she gets to school. There is a big transition program now in Head Start that deals with this need. Many parents take their hands off when the child goes to school. Let the school do it. She is going to learn to read, I do not have to read to her anymore. The school is going to do it. That is why so many children who have been through Head Start regress. They begin to fail. They do not stay stimulated. They do not catch up. It is the parent power—and by parents, we are using the very broad definition—anybody who cares for that child is family if the parents are not able to do it. But the parents if they can, if they are present, they are the most special and important people you can empower.

Second, develop a multicultural consciousness. This is not a white, Anglo-Saxon, Protestant, male-oriented society now, if it ever was. Or even one where the Caucasians will govern.

Finally, mentor and share with those with whom you build coalitions. Get to know them as people. Alice Honig and I have had a wonderful time in just the short time I have known her. She has a 93-year-old mother. I have a 93-year-old mother. We were both born in New York. We already know lots of things about each other. We are going to be friends. This is what you need to do, not just make a cold impersonal phone call. You need to get to know people as people. And when you do that, you will find that they think of you, not just in terms of being the children's librarian, but you are that marvelous person who can help them.

Works Cited

Alter, J. (1993, June 28). Between the lines: The Jurassic park press. *Newsweek,* p. 37.

Carson, R. (1956). *The Sense of Wonder.* New York: Harper & Row.

Mathews, V. H. (1975). *Libraries for today and tomorrow.* New York: Doubleday.

Rockefeller Foundation. (1989). *Literacy and the market place: Improving the literacy of low income single mothers.* New York: The Rockefeller Foundation.

Neddlman, R., & Zuckerman, B. (1992, February). Fight illiteracy: Prescribe a book. *Contemporary Pediatrics,* p. 41–60.

Will, G. F. (1993, Dec. 13). Trickle down culture. *Newsweek,* p. 84.

Roster of Participants
Achieving School Readiness
Institute

Teresa Acosta
Doctoral Student
Early Childhood Education
University of Texas at Austin
Austin, TX

Janice Arcuria
Children's Service Coordinator
Arlington Public Library
    System
Arlington, TX

Noreen Bernstein
Youth Services Director
Williamsburg Regional Library
Williamsburg, VA

Marie E. Bindeman
Youth Services Consultant
NIOGA Library System
Lockport, NY

Bronwyn Booker
Master's Student
University of Texas at Austin
Austin, TX

Inga Boudreau
Youth Services Coordinator
Multnomah County Library
Portland, OR

Pauletta Bracy
Associate Professor, SLIS
North Carolina Central
    University
Durham, NC

Mary Bryant
Director, Office of Early
    Intervention and School
    Readiness
Florida Department of
    Education
Tallahassee, FL

Gwen Chance
Project Director
Texas Head Start Collaboration
    Project
Austin, TX

Oralia Garza de Cortes
Supervising Librarian, Dove
    Springs Branch
Austin Public Library
Austin, TX

Vicky Crosson
Children's Department
    Supervisor
New Haven Public Library
New Haven, CT

Sherry Des Enfants
Youth Services Coordinator
DeKalb County Public
    Library
Decatur, GA

Tresia Dodson
Children's Librarian
Winfield Public Library
Winfield, KS

Frances Dowd
Associate Professor
Texas Woman's University,
    SLIS
Denton, TX

Ellen Fader
Public Library Consultant
Oregon State Library
Salem, OR

Andrew Finkbeiner
Librarian for Youth Services
Rockford Public Library
Rockford, IL

Carole Fiore
Youth Services Consultant
State Library of Florida
Tallahassee, FL

Adrianna Flores
Master's Student
University of Texas at Austin
Austin, TX

Marsha Fowle
Children's Services
    Supervisor
Hampton Public Library
Hampton, VA

Dawn Gardner
Youth Services Librarian,
    Department Head
Flagstaff City—Coconino
    County Public Library
Flagstaff, AZ

Grace Greene
Children's Services Consultant
Vermont Department of
    Libraries
Montpelier, VT

Genie Hammel
Children's Services Librarian
Plano Public Library
Plano, TX

Patricia Hooten
Executive Director
Orange County Child Care
Paoli, IN

Catherine Howser
Library Program Advisor
Arkansas State Library
Little Rock, AR

Mary Jackson
Coordinator of Children's and
    Youth Services
Nebraska Library Commission
Lincoln, NE

Ivonne Jimenez
Extension Services
    Administrator
El Paso Public Library
El Paso, TX

Peggy Kaser
Youth Librarian
Tippecanoe County Public
    Library
Lafayette, IN

Meredith Knight
Master's Student
University of Texas at Austin
Austin, TX

Molly Krukewitt
Coordinator of Youth Services
Fort Bend County Library
Richmond, TX

Jeanette Larson
Manager, Continuing
    Education and Consulting
Texas State Library
Austin, TX

Michele Lauer-Bader
Head, Children's Services
Patchogue-Medford Library
Patchogue, NY

Melanie Lawson
Assistant Director
Dyess AFB Child Development
    Center
Dyess AFB, TX

Anne Lundin
Assistant Professor, SLIS
University of Wisconsin
    at Madison
Madison, WI

Anita McClanahan
Coordinator, Early Childhood
    Education
Oregon Dept. of Education
Salem, OR

Shelley G. McNamara
Associate Professor, CIS
Drexel University
Philadelphia, PA

Penny Markey
Coordinator of Youth Services
County of Los Angeles Public
    Library
Downey, CA

Ruth Metcalf
Children's Services Consultant
Ohio State Library
Columbus, OH

Harriet Miles
Sr. Librarian, Youth Services
    Coordinator
Palmdale City Library
Palmdale, CA

Karen Muskopf
Youth Services Consultant
Illinois State Library
Springfield, IL

Sue McCleaf Nespeca
Youth Services Coordinator
NOLA Regional Library
    System
Warren, OH

Pamela Pirio
Coordinator, Stupp Teacher
    Resource Center
Missouri Botanical Garden
St. Louis, MO

Karen Preuss
Children's Services Consultant
New Mexico State Library
Santa Fe, NM

Jane Roeber
Youth Services Coordinator
Division of Library Services
Wisconsin Dept. of Public
    Instruction
Madison, WI

Marilyn Shelton
Associate Professor
School of Education and
    Human Development
California State University
    at Fresno
Fresno, CA

Paula Sherman
Lead Preschool Teacher
United Front Child
    Development Programs, Inc.
New Bedford, MA

Janice Smuda
Project LEAP Librarian
Cuyahoga County Public
    Library
Parma, OH

Susan Steinfirst
Professor, SLIS
University of North Carolina
    at Chapel Hill
Chapel Hill, NC

Denise J. Swinehart
Head of Children's Services
Lake County Public Library
Merrillville, IN

Kathy Toon
Manager, Children's Center
Dallas Public Library
Dallas, TX

Ann Trujillo
Early Childhood/ Elementary
    Education Consultant
New Mexico Dept. of
    Education
Santa Fe, NM

Virginia Walter
Assistant Professor, GSLIS
University of California at Los
    Angeles
Los Angeles, CA

Caroline Ward
Chief, Youth Services
Nassau Library System
Uniondale, NY

Aisha White
Project Director
Mr. Roger's Neighborhood
    Childcare Partnership
Pittsburgh, PA

Amanda Williams
Doctoral Student
Library and Information
    Science
University of Texas at Austin
Austin, TX

Wendy Woodfill
Children's Services Librarian
Hennepin County Library
Mound, MN

INDEX

Achieving School Readiness
Institute, xiii, 134–138
American Library Association
(ALA), position paper, x
Association for Library Service to
Children (ALSC), 135, 140
*Competencies for Librarians
Serving Children in Public
Libraries,* 135–136, 140
"at-risk" children, 60, 65, 125, 151,
157, 162
Carnegie Corporation Report,
151
creativity and, 5
attachment theorists, 42–44, 61

Carson, Rachel, 152
child rearing, 31–48, 151–153,
156–157 *see also* parenting
styles
children's storytelling, 1–9, 22,
98–102, 123–124 *see also*
emergent literacy; storytelling;
sociocultural influences
classroom play, 17–21
cognitive activity, play as, 11–14,
18–26
and emergent literacy, ix–xii,
14–17, 83–88, 94–95, 98–99,
101–105, 115–118, 121,
123–124
cognitive awareness, 40, 104–105,
113–115, 156–157
cognitive development, xi–xii,
11–16, 21, 52–55, 67–69,
113–115

and cultural diversity, 88–94,
152
and language, 83–88, 104–105
and learning styles, 54–62
and low literacy, *see* low literacy,
effects on children
and reading and writing, 94–106
role of librarian in, 47–48,
76–77, 106, 115–118,
129–130, 141–142
cognitive style, 54–55, 58, 69–74
and creativity, 5, 52, 60–62, 66,
75
and cultural diversity, 65–69
and gender, 62–65
and parenting, 67–69, 104–105,
156–157
recognition of, 5, 74–77
and school readiness, 71–74,
113–115, 137
cognitive tempo, 56–57
construction play, 13 *see also*
Piagetian theory
culturally compatible education,
67–69
cultural diversity, xv, 47, 84–86,
88–94, 98, 135–136, 162
and creativity, 65–69
and language competence, 82–93

developmental play, xiv, 11–21,
128–129, 137
and interpersonal skills, 35–36,
44, 45–46, 53, 55–56
sociocultural aspects, 14–16
diversity, *see* cultural diversity